FRANCIS

THE PEOPLE'S POPE

FRANCIS
THE PEOPLE'S POPE

TED RALL

NEW YORK / OAKLAND / LONDON

A Seven Stories Press First Edition

Seven Stories Press
140 Watts Street
New York, NY 10013
www.sevenstories.com

Library of Congress Cataloging-in-Publication Data

Names: Rall, Ted, author.
Title: Francis : the people's pope / Ted Rall.
Description: First [edition]. | New York : Seven Stories Press, 2018.
Identifiers: LCCN 2018000344 | ISBN 9781609807603 (pbk.)
Subjects: LCSH: Francis, Pope, 1936---Comic books, strips, etc. |
    Popes--Biography. | Graphic novels.
Classification: LCC BX1378.7 .R35 2018 | DDC 282.092 [B] --dc23
LC record available at https://lccn.loc.gov/2018000344

Printed in the USA.

9 8 7 6 5 4 3 2 1

FRANCIS
THE PEOPLE'S POPE

MARCH 13, 2013:
CARDINAL JORGE MARIO BERGOGLIO
REPLACES POPE BENEDICT XVI, WHO
ABDICATED DUE TO DECLINING HEALTH AND
OLD AGE.

REFLECTING HIS HUMILITY AND INTEREST IN
THE POOR, BERGOGLIO CHOOSES THE
NAME FRANCIS, AFTER SAINT FRANCIS OF
ASSISI.

POPE FRANCIS IS THE FIRST POPE
FROM THE ORDER OF THE JESUITS,
KNOWN WITHIN THE ROMAN CATHOLIC
CHURCH FOR ITS DEVOTION TO
SCIENCE AND OTHER SCHOLARLY
PURSUITS.

AS AN ARGENTINE, HE IS BOTH THE FIRST POPE FROM THE AMERICAS AND THE FIRST FROM THE SOUTHERN HEMISPHERE.

HE IS ALSO THE FIRST NON-EUROPEAN
POPE SINCE GREGORY III, A SYRIAN,
WHO DIED IN 741.

MANY CATHOLICS WELCOME POPE FRANCIS AS A BREATH OF FRESH AIR AFTER THE DECREPIT AND CONSERVATIVE BENEDICT AND HIS PREDECESSOR, JOHN PAUL II, ALSO A CONSERVATIVE.

FRANCIS TELLS INTERVIEWERS THAT HIS PAPACY WILL BE OPEN, LIBERAL, AND FOCUSED ON THE PROBLEMS OF THE POOR.

THE CHURCH... IS THE HOME OF ALL, NOT A SMALL CHAPEL THAT CAN ONLY HOLD A SMALL GROUP...

HE SIGNALS THIS SHIFT TO THE LEFT BY MOVING INTO THE DOMUS SANCTAE MARTHAE GUESTHOUSE INSTEAD OF THE APOSTOLIC PALACE USED BY HIS PREDECESSORS, WEARING VESTMENTS WITHOUT ORNAMENTATION, AND REQUESTING A SILVER RATHER THAN GOLD PAPAL "FISHERMAN'S" RING.

MITER

PAPAL FERULA

PALLIUM

CHASUBLE

FASCIA

FISHER-MAN'S RING

CASSOCK

THOUGH CRITICAL OF MARXISM, HE IS AT LEAST AS CONCERNED ABOUT THE PAIN CAUSED BY CAPITALISM IN GENERAL AND CONSUMERISM IN PARTICULAR. THIS MIDDLE GROUND GUIDES HIS VIEWS ABOUT ECONOMICS.

" Some people continue to defend trickle-down theories which assume that economic growth, encouraged by a free market, will inevitably succeed in bringing about greater justice and inclusiveness in the world. This opinion... [is] crude and naïve..."

FRANCIS MAKES GOOD ON HIS PROMISE TO BE A BREATH OF FRESH AIR ON ISSUES OF PERSONAL IDENTITY AND TO CLEAN HOUSE ON TWO MAJOR SCANDALS. FIRST, HE INVESTIGATES AND REFORMS THE VATICAN BANK, WHICH HAS BEEN PLAGUED BY CORRUPTION AND MONEY LAUNDERING.

THEN HE TAKES ON THE ISSUE OF PEDOPHILE PRIESTS. FOR DECADES, CHURCH OFFICIALS HAVE STONEWALLED AND DENIED WRONGDOING, COVERING UP PRIESTS' DEPREDATIONS BY MOVING THEM AROUND FROM PARISH TO PARISH. FRANCIS MEETS WITH THE VICTIMS AND THEIR REPRESENTATIVES, ORDERS PAYOUTS, AND FIRES OFFICIALS IMPLICATED IN COVER-UPS.

The New York Times

EUROPE

On Gay Priests, Pope Francis Asks, 'Who Am I to Judge?'

Pope Francis: Who am I to judge gay people?

IDEAS RELIGION

The Pope Francis Statement That Changed the Church on LGBT Issues

ONE OF HIS STATEMENTS SENDS A CLEAR SIGNAL ABOUT WHO HE IS AND WHAT HE BELIEVES. ASKED ABOUT GAY PEOPLE, FRANCIS REPLIES: "WHO AM I TO JUDGE THEM IF THEY'RE SEEKING THE LORD IN GOOD FAITH?"

THIS IS ALL PROMISING. BUT MANY WONDER IF FRANCIS IS TOO LITTLE, TOO LATE. IN THE WESTERN WORLD, THE CATHOLIC CHURCH IS LOSING MEMBERS, MONEY, AND POLITICAL INFLUENCE.

YOU HAVE ONLY TO LOOK AT PRESIDENT OBAMA TO SEE WHAT HAPPENS WHEN SOARING ORATORY FAILS TO MATERIALIZE IN REAL TERMS THAT CHANGE PEOPLE'S LIVES.

OVER THE NEXT FEW YEARS, HOWEVER, FRANCIS ISSUES STATEMENTS THAT WERE FORMERLY UNTHINKABLE.

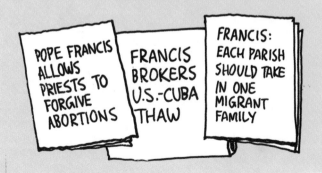

GENERALLY, IT IS TRUE --
WORDS AREN'T ENOUGH.
BUT MAYBE THAT'S
DIFFERENT WHEN YOU'RE
POPE.

CATECHISM

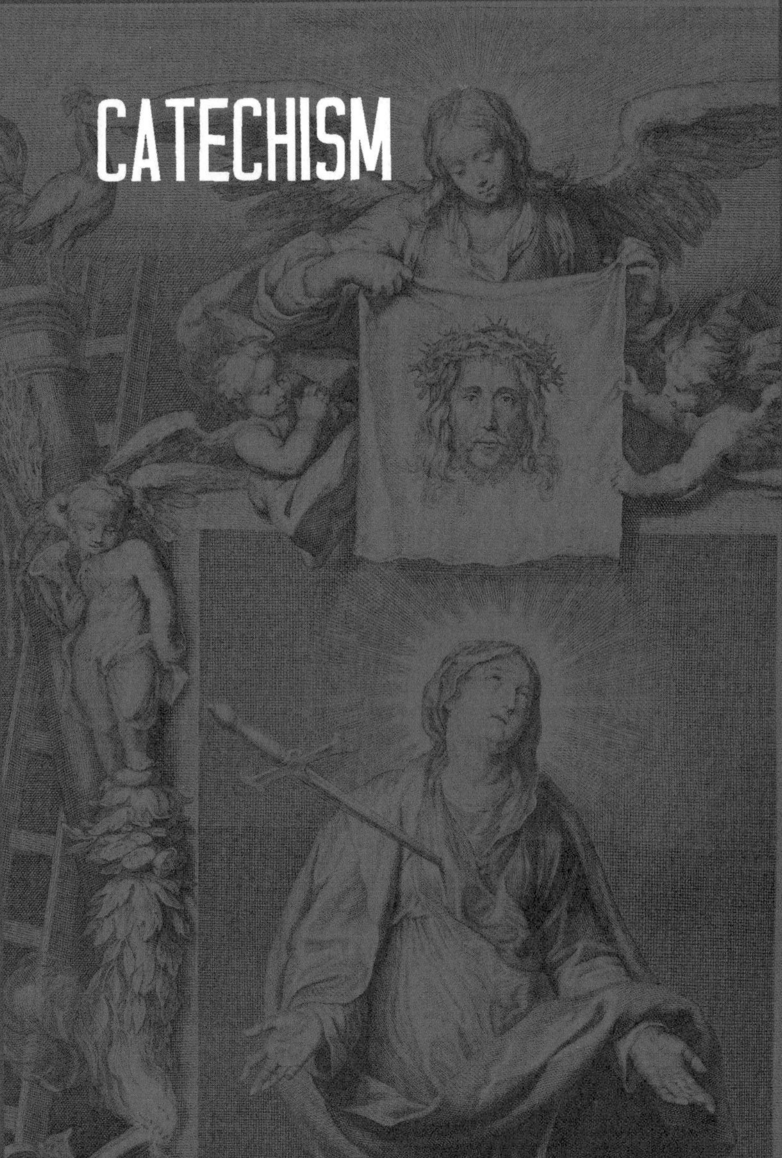

THREE BIG ATTRIBUTES DISTINGUISH
ROMAN CATHOLICISM FROM THE OTHER
MAJOR CHRISTIAN DENOMINATIONS.

Also-rans:

RESTORATIONISM &
NON-TRINITARIANISM
CHURCH OF THE EAST

FIRST: CATHOLICISM CAME FIRST.

BY DOGMA AND BY TRADITION,
CATHOLICS CONSIDER THEIRS TO BE
THE OLDEST CHRISTIAN CHURCH,
FOUNDED BY JESUS AND RULED BY A
CONTINUOUS RUN OF PONTIFFS
DATING BACK TO SAINT PETER, WHO IS
CONSIDERED TO BE THE FIRST BISHOP
OF ROME.

TRADITION AND HISTORY, HOWEVER, ARE NOT ALWAYS THE SAME. BISHOPS MAY NOT HAVE EXISTED UNTIL THE SECOND CENTURY.

JESUS'S APOSTLE PETER MAY NEVER HAVE EVEN VISITED ROME.

Nope. Didn't happen.

SINCE AT LEAST THE COUNTER-REFORMATION OF THE 1500s, CATHOLICISM HAS MAINTAINED EXPLICIT OPPOSITION TO MAJOR INSTITUTIONAL AND THEOLOGICAL REFORMS -- INDEED, THAT OPPOSITION CURRENTLY CONTINUES TO DIVIDE THE CATHOLIC CHURCH FROM NEARLY HALF OF ALL FOLLOWERS OF CHRISTIANITY.

HISTORY AND TRUTH, IT SEEMS, ARE NOT ALWAYS THE SAME EITHER.

SECOND: THE CATHOLIC CHURCH HAS LONG POSSESSED THE ORGANIZATIONAL AND POLITICAL CHARACTERISTICS OF A NATION-STATE.

THIS WAS ALSO ARGUABLY TRUE OF ISLAM BEFORE THE CALIPHATE WAS ABOLISHED IN 1924, BUT WHILE POLITICAL ISLAM HAS DEGENERATED, POLITICAL CATHOLICISM RETAINS ITS POWER AND INFLUENCE. ALONG WITH ITS TWO-THOUSAND-YEAR HISTORY -- FAR MORE ENDURING THAN MOST EMPIRES -- CATHOLICISM AS A POLITICAL ENTITY LENDS ITS LEADERS MORE INFLUENCE THAN THE AUTHORITY OF MINISTERS OF THE VARIOUS PROTESTANT DENOMINATIONS.

THE ROMAN CATHOLIC CHURCH IS ARGUABLY MORE POWERFUL THAN ANY NATION-STATE. IT IS MORE LIKE AN EMPIRE WHOSE INFLUENCE IS PERVASIVE BUT DISCREET. THE CATHOLIC CHURCH HAS REDRAWN NATIONAL BORDERS, CONFERRED LEGITIMACY UPON (AND WITHHELD IT FROM) FOREIGN HEADS OF STATE, AND REPEATEDLY SPARKED WARS THAT KILLED MILLIONS.

The crowning of Holy Roman Emperor Charles V by Pope Clement VII, 1520

EVEN IN ITS CURRENTLY DIMINISHED FORM, VATICAN CITY IS MORE THAN A COUNTRY UNTO ITSELF.

ROMAN CATHOLICS WORLDWIDE COULD BE SAID TO COMPRISE THE WORLD'S LARGEST POLITICAL GROUP, JOINED BY THEIR FAITH.

THE POPE IS A HEAD OF STATE.

THE THIRD DISTINGUISHING CHARACTERISTIC OF THE CHURCH IS PENANCE. CATHOLICS BELIEVE THEY CAN PRAY FOR FORGIVENESS AND RECEIVE ABSOLUTION OF THEIR SINS FROM GOD IN EXCHANGE FOR MAKING RESTITUTION AND/OR ACCEPTING PUNISHMENT VIA A PRIEST ADMINISTERING THIS SACRAMENT:

"I CONFESS TO ALMIGHTY GOD AND TO YOU, FATHER, THAT I HAVE SINNED. MY LAST CONFESSION WAS __ WEEKS (MONTHS, YEARS) AGO...

FOR [THE SINS I COMMITTED DURING THIS TIME] AND ALL THE SINS THAT I HAVE COMMITTED DURING MY LIFE, I AM DEEPLY SORRY."

IT WOULD BE HARD TO OVERSTATE HOW THE SYSTEMIC APPLICATION FOR AND RECEIPT OF CONFESSION SEPARATES CATHOLICISM FROM PROTESTANTISM. (THOUGH THE EASTERN ORTHODOX CHURCH SHARES WITH ROME ITS BELIEF IN THE POWER OF PENANCE.)

IN THE UNITED STATES, MANY PROTESTANT
DENOMINATIONS FOLLOW THE TRADITION
ESTABLISHED DURING THE REFORMATION BY
THE INFLUENTIAL PASTOR AND THEOLOGIAN
JOHN CALVIN. INFLUENCED BY THE
AUGUSTINIAN VIEW THAT HUMANITY IS
INESCAPABLY PREDISPOSED TO EVIL, THIS
SIXTEENTH-CENTURY FRENCHMAN BELIEVED
THAT HUMAN BEINGS WERE SUBJECT TO
"TOTAL DEPRAVITY," IN WHICH EVERY HUMAN
ACTION IS MIXED WITH EVIL, WHETHER OR NOT
THEY ARE OUTWARDLY GOOD OR BAD.
ACCORDING TO CALVIN, GOD ALONE
INITIATES AND CARRIES THROUGH
SALVATION -- PEOPLE ARE PREDESTINED TO
EITHER ETERNAL LIFE OR ETERNAL DAMNATION.

MODERN AMERICAN PROTESTANTISM HAS
EVOLVED BEYOND CALVINISM, BUT THE
INFLUENCE OF CALVIN'S VISION OF
HUMANITY'S IRREDEEMABLE SINFULNESS HAS
HAD DEEP ROOTS IN THE US SINCE AT LEAST
THE PURITAN MIGRATION.

THE VENGEFUL, PUNITIVE JUDGE OF HUMANITY
ENVISIONED BY 1700s NEW ENGLAND
PREACHER AND THEOLOGIAN JONATHAN
EDWARDS REMAINS RELEVANT TO MUCH "FIRE
AND BRIMSTONE" PROTESTANT PREACHING IN
AMERICA TODAY:

"The God that holds you over the pit of hell, much as one holds a spider or some loathsome insect over the fire, abhors you, and is dreadfully provoked. His wrath towards you burns like fire; he looks upon you as worthy of nothing else but to be cast into the fire. He is of purer eyes than to bear you in his sight; you are ten thousand times as abominable in his eyes as the most hateful, venomous serpent is in ours."

— *"Sinners in the Hands of an Angry God" (1741)*

CATHOLICS, ON THE OTHER HAND, TAKE COMFORT IN THEIR BELIEF THAT EVERYONE CAN BE FORGIVEN FOR THEIR SINS, NO MATTER HOW EGREGIOUS.

FOR CATHOLICS, SALVATION IS ATTAINABLE THROUGH HUMAN ACTION.

NOT SURPRISINGLY, OUTSIDERS (AND NOT A FEW OF THE FAITHFUL) HAVE TAKEN NOTE OF THE TEMPTATION TO VIEW THE SACRAMENT OF PENANCE AS A SORT OF "GET OUT OF JAIL FREE" CARD THAT ELIMINATES MORAL HAZARD BECAUSE COMMITTING A SIN DOESN'T HAVE TO RESULT IN ETERNAL DAMNATION.

OTHER CRITICS TAKE THE OPPOSITE TACK:

"Whether things are good or bad, or you're simply eating tacos in the park, there is always the crushing guilt."
—Jack Donaghy, character played by Alec Baldwin in the TV show *30 Rock*

THE PSYCHOLOGICAL MAFIA DRAMA *THE SOPRANOS* EXPLORED THIS PARADOX IN AN EPISODE IN WHICH THE MOB BOSS'S WIFE ASKED HER PRIEST ABOUT ACCEPTING "BLOOD MONEY" IN THE FORM OF JEWELRY AND LIFE IN A BIG HOUSE:

EASY WAY OUT? OR TRUE TO CHRIST'S ADMONITION THAT NO ONE IS WITHOUT SIN SO EVERYONE DESERVES TO RECEIVE MERCY?

EITHER WAY, FORGIVENESS AND COMPASSION ARE AT THE HEART OF WHAT IT MEANS TO BE CATHOLIC.

BY ITS OWN ACCOUNT, THE
CATHOLIC CHURCH HAS
COMMITTED MANY MISTAKES
AND CRIMES.

THERE WAS NEITHER
CONFRONTATION,
NOR CRITICISM, NOR
A PLEA FOR JUSTICE.

John Morely,
author of
Vatican Diplomacy
and the Jews
during the
Holocaust, 1939-
1943, about
Pope Pius XII's
friendly relations
with Nazi
Germany

SINCE AT LEAST 1610, AFTER EXTENSIVE
USE OF EXPERIMENTS TO VALIDATE HIS
ASTRONOMICAL THEORIES, GALILEO GALILEI
DETERMINED DEFINITIVELY THAT THE EARTH
REVOLVES AROUND THE SUN.

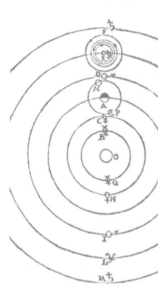

AFTER NEARLY TWO
DECADES OF INFLICTING
VARYING DEGREES OF
OSTRACISM, THE
CATHOLIC CHURCH,
THROUGH THE ROMAN
INQUISITION, THREATENED
GALILEO WITH TORTURE
FOR PUTTING UP ANY
DEFENSE OF SCIENTIFIC
IDEAS CONTRARY TO
CHURCH DOCTRINE. HE
AGREED TO RENOUNCE HIS
BELIEF IN HELIOCENTRICITY,
AND IN 1633 HE WAS
CONVICTED OF A
"STRONG SUSPICION OF
HERESY" AND HIS WRITINGS
WERE BANNED.

ALL THE SAME,
IT MOVES.

SOMETIMES, HOWEVER, CHURCH OFFICIALS DO REVERSE COURSE.

IN 1992, CENTURIES AFTER GALILEO'S DEATH, POPE JOHN PAUL II OFFICIALLY DECLARED AT THE PONTIFICAL ACADEMY OF SCIENCES THAT GALILEO HAD BEEN RIGHT ALL ALONG. THE CHURCH, HE CONCEDED, HAD BEEN WRONG.

The New York Times

After 350 Years, Vatican Says Galileo Was Right: It Moves

Los Angeles Times

Earth Moves for Vatican in Galileo Case

New Scientist

Vatican admits Galileo was right

Now there's a Vatican Observatory at the Pope's summer residence, Castel Gandolfo.

THIS COMBINATION OF A HIERARCHICAL POLITICAL BUREAUCRACY WITH A CULTURE OF REPENTANCE AND FORGIVENESS HAS ALLOWED THE CATHOLIC CHURCH TO OPERATE WITH REMARKABLE FLEXIBILITY.

IT GAVE THE TWO-THOUSAND-YEAR-OLD CHURCH THE CHANCE TO COME TO GRIPS WITH MODERNITY, AND TO ADAPT MORE EFFECTIVELY THAN MUCH YOUNGER RELIGIOUS INSTITUTIONS -- ALBEIT MORE THAN A LITTLE BELATEDLY, AS IN THE CASE OF GALILEO.

Stephen Jay Gould

SINCERE CHRISTIANS MUST NOW ACCEPT EVOLUTION NOT MERELY AS A PLAUSIBLE POSSIBILITY BUT ALSO AS AN EFFECTIVELY PROVEN FACT.

-Reaction to Pope John II's 1996 statement accepting evolution

AS WITH MANY ASPECTS OF RELIGION, THIS
BOON COMES AT A COST. THE CHURCH'S
CULTURE OF FORGIVENESS AND REDEMPTION
CONVENIENTLY APPLIES TO ITSELF. WHEN IT
SCREWS UP, AS IT DID THROUGHOUT THE
PEDOPHILE PRIEST SCANDAL, THE
BUREAUCRACY HAS A TENDENCY TO
PROTECT ITS INSIDERS, MAKE EXCUSES, AND
DISMISS VICTIMS AS OUTSIDERS. AT THESE
TIMES, CHURCH OFFICIALS SEEM TO FORGET
THAT THERE IS NO REDEMPTION WITHOUT
MEANINGFUL PENANCE.

Boston Sunday Globe

LOTTERY, PAGE A2
Volume 261
Number 6
$2.00

JANUARY 6, 2002

...llowed abuse by priest for years

Priest John J. Geoghan leaving his
...ine in Scituate in November

LET HE WHO IS WITHOUT SIN
CAST THE FIRST STONE... [BE]
INDULGENT TOWARDS SINNERS
AND PRAY TO GOD TO ASK
FOR FORGIVENESS FOR
OUR FAILINGS.

—Pope Benedict XVI,
pontificating on the
Gospel of John to urge
forgiveness of church
actions and inactions
in the child sex abuse
scandal

40

ARGUABLY THE GREATEST CRISIS IN CATHOLIC HISTORY WAS PROMPTED BY THE PROTESTANT REFORMATION'S CRITICISMS OF CHURCH CORRUPTION.

THE SIXTEENTH-CENTURY COUNCIL OF TRENT MANAGED TO RESPOND TO THE UPHEAVAL, RELEGITIMIZING THE CHURCH AND SETTING THE STAGE FOR MODEST REFORMS IN RESPONSE TO SOME OF MARTIN LUTHER'S COMPLAINTS, INCLUDING THE ABOLITION OF THE SALE OF INDULGENCES.

VATICAN II

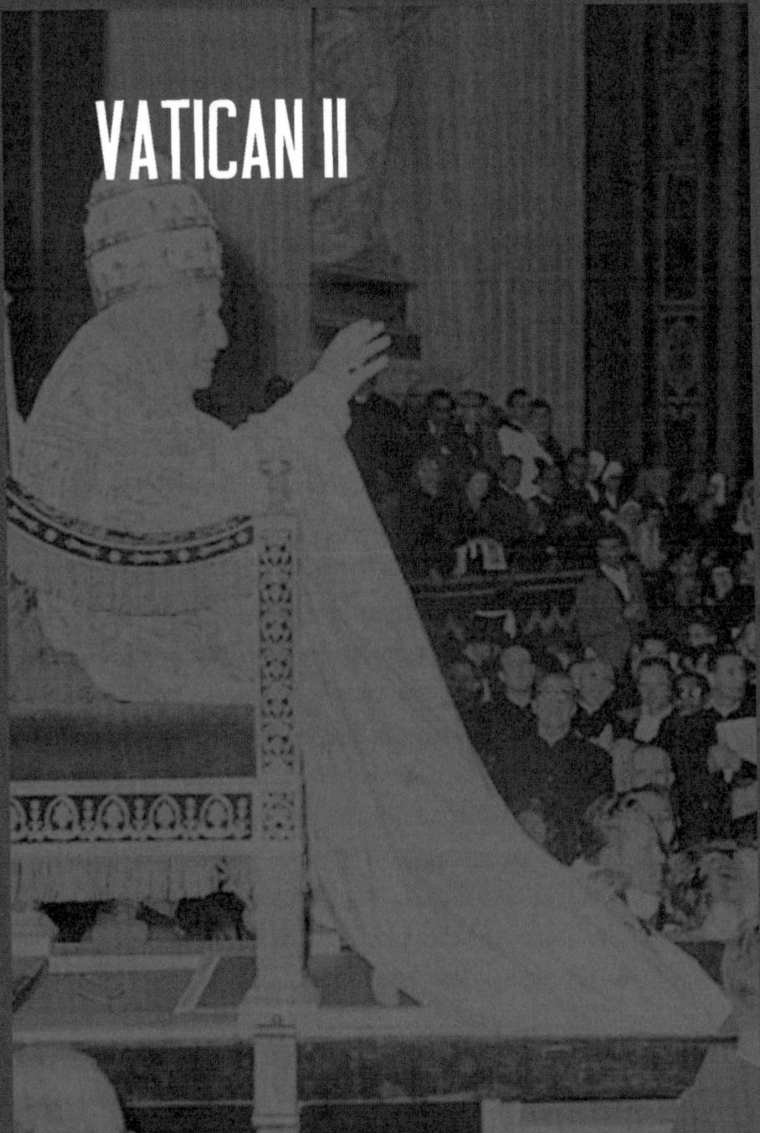

ECUMENICAL COUNCILS ARE MEETINGS OF PATRIARCHS, CARDINALS, BISHOPS, ABBOTS, MALE LEADERS OF RELIGIOUS ORDERS, AND OTHER FIGURES NOMINATED BY THE POPE. THE COUNCILS DEBATE ISSUES AND CONTROVERSIES OVER FAITH AND CHURCH DISCIPLINE. DECISIONS ARE ULTIMATELY RATIFIED BY THE POPE, AND PUBLISHED FOR THE FAITHFUL.

THERE HAVE BEEN TWENTY-ONE SUCH COUNCILS OVER THE SPAN OF 1,700 YEARS.

THE MOST RECENT WAS THE SECOND
VATICAN COUNCIL (BECAUSE IT WAS THE
SECOND TO BE HELD AT THE VATICAN).
SHORTENED BY THE PRESS TO THE POPULAR
NICKNAME "VATICAN II," THE REFORMIST
POPES JOHN XXIII AND PAUL VI PRESIDED
FROM 1962 TO 1965 OVER A SERIES OF
ATTEMPTS TO BRING CATHOLICISM, IF NOT
EXACTLY INTO THE TWENTIETH CENTURY,
CLOSER THAN IT HAD BEEN PREVIOUSLY.

OPEN THE
WINDOWS [OF
THE CHURCH]
AND LET IN
SOME FRESH
AIR.

Pope John XXIII

AMONG THE CHANGES INSTITUTED BY THE SECOND VATICAN COUNCIL:

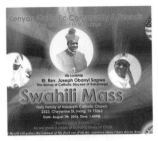

MASS COULD BE SAID IN LOCAL LANGUAGES AND DIALECTS, NOT JUST LATIN

TRADITIONAL CHURCH MUSIC AND IMAGERY COULD BE REPLACED WITH MODERN/POP INFLUENCES

DIVORCED PEOPLE COULD CONTINUE TO RECEIVE COMMUNION

REMARRIAGE WOULD NO LONGER RESULT IN EXCOMMUNICATION

LIBERALIZATION AND MODERNISM WERE THE ORDER OF THE DAY AFTER VATICAN II.

Peter A. Huff
Xavier University

PRIOR TO THIS TIME, THE CHURCH HAD ALMOST BEEN SEEN AS A FORTRESS, VERY MUCH CONCERNED **ABOUT** ITS OWN INTERNAL STABILITY AND INTEGRITY AND ENGAGING THE WORLD IN TERMS OF MISSIONARY ACTIVITY. POPE JOHN WANTED... THE CHURCH [TO] ENGAGE IN ALL THE FORCES OF THE **MODERN WORLD**.

FORMERLY SHUNNED DIVORCEES RETURNED TO MASS TO TAKE COMMUNION DURING THE 1960s. (MY MOTHER WAS ONE OF THEM. HER PARISH PRIEST INVITED HER BACK.)

LATIN MASS, UNDERSTOOD BY FEW OF THE
PARISHIONERS WHO ROTELY RECITED
PRAYERS IN LATIN, WAS ABOLISHED BY FIAT.
MEANWHILE, THE FREEDOM MOVEMENTS OF
THE 1960s SWEPT ACROSS WESTERN
SOCIETIES.

THE 1970s MARKED THE PEAK OF BABY
BOOMER-CENTRIC YOUTH CULTURE. IN ORDER
TO ATTRACT YOUNG WORSHIPERS, MANY
DIOCESES (LOCAL ADMINISTRATIVE
REGIONS) INTRODUCED "MODERN"
CEREMONIES THAT INCLUDED FOLK AND
EVEN ROCK SONGS IN THEIR CHURCHES
PRESIDED OVER BY PRIESTS, SOME WEARING
NORMAL STREET CLOTHES.

THOUGH ITS ROOTS TRACE BACK TO THE 1950s, IT WAS DURING THE 1970s THAT LEFT-LEANING "LIBERATION THEOLOGY" SPREAD FROM LATIN AMERICA INTO AFRICA AND ASIA.

ADHERENTS OF LIBERATION THEOLOGY REMINDED CATHOLICS OF CHRIST'S TEACHING THAT IT IS EASIER FOR A CAMEL TO PASS THROUGH THE EYE OF A NEEDLE THAN FOR A RICH MAN TO ENTER THE KINGDOM OF HEAVEN.

Liberation theology was especially popular in Latin America and sub-Saharan Africa. Euro-centric images of Jesus were modified to make him more relatable.

THEY NEVER SAID IT ALOUD. BUT THEY DIDN'T HAVE TO. THE WAY THEY READ THE BIBLE, MARXISM WASN'T JUST SIMILAR TO CHRISTIANITY. JESUS CHRIST WAS A COMMUNIST.

HE WHO BETRAYS THE POOR BETRAYS **CHRIST**.

Fidel Castro
1959

THAT WAS THE JESUS LIBERATION THEOLOGIANS PREACHED: RADICAL, ANTI-JUDGMENTAL (EXCEPT AGAINST THE RICH), DEVOTED TO THE POOR AND OPPRESSED.

LIBERATION THEOLOGY WASN'T OFFICIAL VATICAN DOGMA. BUT IT WAS THE MOST DYNAMIC STRAIN OF CATHOLIC POLITICS OF THE 1970s AND 1980s. IT WAS TOLERATED BY THE IMMEDIATE POST-VATICAN II PAPACY AND WIDELY VIEWED AS THE FUTURE OF THE CHURCH.

IN THEIR EVERYDAY DECISION MAKING, CATHOLICS WERE URGED TO GIVE "PREFERENTIAL OPTION FOR THE POOR" [SIC]. THE WELL-BEING OF THE POOR AND POWERLESS WAS CONSIDERED TO BE A PRIORITY FOR GOD AS WELL AS BELIEVERS.

"[THE CHRISTIAN FAITHFUL] ARE ALSO OBLIGED TO PROMOTE SOCIAL JUSTICE AND, MINDFUL OF THE PRECEPT OF THE LORD, TO ASSIST THE POOR FROM THEIR OWN RE-SOURCES."

--CATHOLIC CANON LAW 222, §2

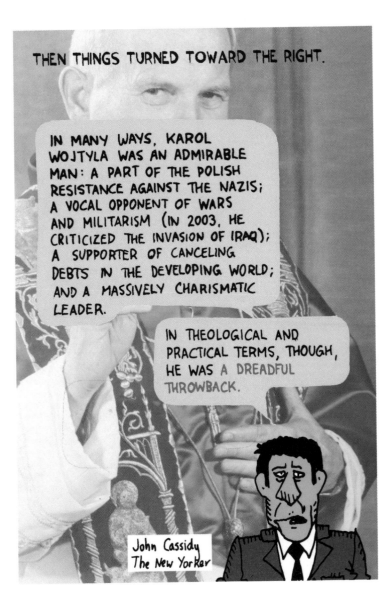

THEN THINGS TURNED TOWARD THE RIGHT.

IN MANY WAYS, KAROL WOJTYLA WAS AN ADMIRABLE MAN: A PART OF THE POLISH RESISTANCE AGAINST THE NAZIS; A VOCAL OPPONENT OF WARS AND MILITARISM (IN 2003, HE CRITICIZED THE INVASION OF IRAQ); A SUPPORTER OF CANCELING DEBTS IN THE DEVELOPING WORLD; AND A MASSIVELY CHARISMATIC LEADER.

IN THEOLOGICAL AND PRACTICAL TERMS, THOUGH, HE WAS A DREADFUL THROWBACK.

John Cassidy
The New Yorker

JOHN PAUL II, THE ANTI-FRANCIS

JOHN PAUL II ASCENDED TO THE PAPACY IN 1978.

A PRODUCT OF THE EXTREMELY CONSERVATIVE, MILITANTLY ANTI-COMMUNIST POLISH CHURCH, JOHN PAUL USED HIS UNDENIABLE ENERGY AND CHARM TO DELIVER A MESSAGE THAT -- TO THOSE WHO PAID CLOSE ATTENTION -- REVERSED OR FROZE MANY OF THE REFORMS OF VATICAN II. BUT NOT THAT MANY CATHOLICS PAID ATTENTION.

FREEDOM CONSISTS NOT IN DOING WHAT WE LIKE, BUT IN HAVING THE RIGHT TO DO WHAT WE **OUGHT**.

IT'S RECENT HISTORY. YET MANY NON-CATHOLICS EITHER NEVER INTERNALIZED OR HAVE FORGOTTEN THAT POLITICALLY JOHN PAUL II WAS, BY MOST MEASURES, A CONSERVATIVE.

GRASSROOTS CHURCH GROUPS WHICH HAD COME INTO BEING IN SOUTH AMERICA CHARACTERIZED BY AUTONOMY AND THE PROTECTION OF THE...POOR WERE ISOLATED AND EVEN DESTROYED IN SOME CASES.

PRIESTS WHO SIDED WITH THEM WERE REMOVED AND FORBIDDEN ACCESS TO COMMUNITY FACILITIES, AND OCCASIONALLY NEW GROUPS WERE SET UP UNDER THE SAME NAME...

– François Houtard in *Le Monde Diplomatique*, on Pope John Paul II's attacks on liberation theology in Latin America during the 1980s

IT WOULD BE A STRETCH TO PUT JOHN PAUL II IN THE SAME CATEGORY AS MARGARET THATCHER OR RONALD REAGAN, THE RIGHT-WING NATIONAL LEADERS WHO HELPED DEFINE THE CONSERVATIVE COUNTERREVOLUTIONS IN THE UK AND US DURING THE LATE 1970s AND 1980s. UNLIKE THATCHER AND REAGAN, JOHN PAUL WAS DEEPLY CONCERNED ABOUT THE OPPRESSED.

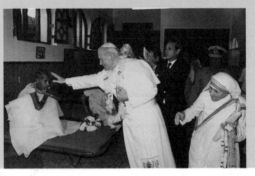

BUT HE WAS ESTABLISHMENTARIAN. JOHN PAUL EVEN RECEIVED REGULAR BRIEFINGS FROM REAGAN'S HEAD OF THE CIA.

John Paul II with Ronald Reagan

PROGRESSIVISM WANED. POPULISM REPLACED IT. JOHN PAUL II EMBRACED VATICAN II'S REMINDER THAT EVERY LAYPERSON IS HOLY, NOT JUST PRIESTS AND NUNS.

BUT PRESENTED WITH MANY OPPORTUNITIES TO TAKE A STAND AGAINST INJUSTICE IN FAVOR OF HUMAN DIGNITY, HE MISSED THEM.

TO BE FAIR, IT'S HIGHLY UNLIKELY THAT EITHER TRADITION OR DOGMA WOULD HAVE ALLOWED ANY POPE TO YIELD FOR THE CHURCH TO ENDORSE -- AS HIS CRITICS DEMANDED -- ABORTION RIGHTS, BIRTH CONTROL, OR GAY MARRIAGE.

A NATION THAT KILLS ITS OWN CHILDREN IS A NATION WITHOUT HOPE.

STILL, THE TWENTY-SIX-YEAR-LONG PAPACY OF THIS PRODUCT OF THE TRADITIONALIST, ANTI-COMMUNIST POLISH CATHOLIC CHURCH WAS DEFINED BY HOLDING THE LINE AGAINST REFORM -- AND REVERSING LIBERAL GAINS.

ONLY THE CHASTE MAN AND THE CHASTE WOMAN ARE CAPABLE OF **REAL LOVE**.

ONE THING JOHN PAUL RARELY DID WAS THINK OUTSIDE THE BOX. THERE IS, FOR EXAMPLE, NO PROHIBITION IN THE BIBLE AGAINST WOMEN BEING ORDAINED AS PRIESTS.

INDEED, WOMEN PRIESTS SERVED MASS IN THE EARLY CHURCH AND A WOMAN DEACON IS MENTIONED IN THE GOSPEL.

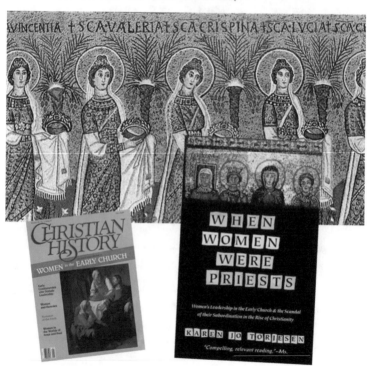

YET JOHN PAUL II NEVER SERIOUSLY ENTERTAINED THE SUGGESTION OF ORDAINING WOMEN TO THE PRIESTHOOD, AND DISMISSED IT WITHOUT THE THOUGHTFUL CONSIDERATION DEMANDED BY NUNS AND WOMEN LAY WORSHIPERS.

...I DECLARE THAT THE CHURCH HAS NO AUTHORITY WHATSOEVER TO CONFER PRIESTLY ORDINATION ON WOMEN...

1994

Apostolic Letter *Ordinatio Sacerdotalis* ON RESERVING PRIESTLY ORDINATION TO MEN ALONE

WOMEN COULDN'T BE PRIESTS BECAUSE WOMEN COULDN'T BE PRIESTS. Q.E.D.

TO LIBERAL CATHOLICS, ESPECIALLY IN THE
US, SOME OF THE NEW PONTIFF'S
POSITIONS FELT RETROGRADE AND OUT OF
TOUCH WITH MODERNITY.

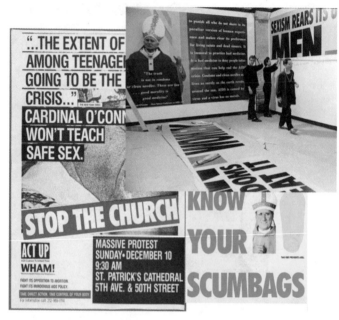

EVEN AS THE GLOBAL AIDS EPIDEMIC OF THE
1980s WAS KILLING HUNDREDS OF
THOUSANDS, JOHN PAUL II STRIDENTLY
OPPOSED THE USE OF CONDOMS AS BIRTH
CONTROL. OFFICIAL CHURCH POLICY SEEMED
HEARTLESS AND STUPID IN THE FACE OF SO
MUCH MISERY.

TO MAKE THINGS WORSE, AFTER
PERCOLATING FOR DECADES, THE STORY
BROKE DURING JOHN PAUL II'S PAPACY THAT
PRIESTS AND OTHER CHURCH OFFICIALS HAD
BETRAYED THEIR POSITIONS IN THEIR
COMMUNITIES BY RAPING THOUSANDS OF
CHILDREN, MOSTLY BOYS, AT CHURCH AND
AT PAROCHIAL SCHOOLS FOR YEARS -- AND
REPEATEDLY GOTTEN AWAY WITH IT.

A GOLDEN OLYMPICS FOR THE U.S.A.

Newsweek

March 4, 2002

SEX, SHAME AND THE CATHOLIC CHURCH

80 Priests Accused of
Child Abuse in Boston—
And New Soul-Searching
Across America

...art of 'Windtalkers,' Living

World-Herald

...PER OWNED BY EMPLOYEES

SUNRISE EDITION
SATURDAY, JUNE 15, 200...

...ury awards $800,000 for abuse

Omaha Archdiocese owes an ex-altar
...0,000 and his mother $50,000.

Bishops vote to oust sex abusers

EXTRA EDITION

The Boston Globe
FRIDAY, DECEMBER 13, 2002

Cardinal Law resigns

Church looks
to future free

In letter, he states:
'I both apologize
and beg forgiveness'

EVEN MORE SHAMEFULLY THAN WITH THE AIDS CRISIS, JOHN PAUL II'S FIRST INSTINCT WHEN REACTING TO THE PEDOPHILE PRIEST SCANDAL IN THE UNITED STATES, IRELAND, AUSTRALIA, AND ELSEWHERE WAS TO PROTECT THE CHURCH RATHER THAN ITS MANY VICTIMS.

Caught raping kids in this parish?

No problem! The Church simply transfered you to **ANOTHER ONE**!

INDEED, HE HAD A TERRIBLE RECORD, FULL OF DENIAL AND FOOT-DRAGGING, ON THE GREATEST CRISIS TO CONFRONT THE CATHOLIC CHURCH SINCE THE REFORMATION OF THE 16TH CENTURY.

Richard McBrien
University of Notre Dame
theologian

THE CHURCH ASSUMED A DEFENSIVE POSTURE.
IT MINIMIZED THE HARM DONE, ATTEMPTED TO
DISCREDIT ACCUSERS, AND STALLED CIVIL
LAWSUITS WITH AGGRESSIVE LEGAL DEFENSES.

DISGUSTED AT THE CHASM BETWEEN THE
INSTITUTION'S LOFTY LANGUAGE AND
CORRUPT ACTION, MANY CATHOLICS DRIFTED
AWAY FROM THE CHURCH.

WHY DID IT HAPPEN? SOME SAY IT'S A MATTER OF OPPORTUNISM, THAT PRIESTS SIMPLY HAD TOO MUCH ACCESS, ONE-ON-ONE, TO CHILDREN. JOHN CORNWELL'S BOOK *THE DARK BOX* BLAMES A 1910 DECREE ISSUED BY POPE PIUS X SAYING THAT CONFESSION SHOULD BEGIN AT AGE SEVEN.

CORNWELL NOTES HOW SCHEMING ABUSERS USED THE PRIVACY OF THE CONFESSIONAL TO GROOM KIDS FOR LATER MOLESTATION, OR, INDEED, TO ABUSE THEM RIGHT THERE AND THEN.

ABUSIVE RELATIONSHIPS BETWEEN CLERIC AND CHILD HAVE ALMOST INVARIABLY BEGUN AS A CONTINUATION OF THE **SACRAMENT OF CONFESSION**.

THINGS GOT WORSE, CORNWELL ARGUES, WHEN CONFESSION MOVED TO TWO PEOPLE IN A ROOM BY THEMSELVES.

OTHERS BLAMED THE CRISIS IN PART ON THE CELIBACY REQUIREMENT FOR CLERGY. TENS OF THOUSANDS OF PRIESTS AND NUNS HAVE LEFT THE CHURCH OVER THE LAST FORTY YEARS, MOSTLY TO MARRY.

YOU MAY KISS THE BRIDE.

BUT AGAIN, DESPITE HAVING THE POWER TO WAIVE THE REQUIREMENT FOR THE POTENTIAL BENEFIT OF THE CHURCH AND ITS FOLLOWERS, JOHN PAUL STUCK TO A "BUT THIS IS THE WAY WE'VE ALWAYS DONE IT" POSTURE RATHER THAN OPEN HIS MIND TO NEW WAYS OF LOOKING AT OLD TRADITIONS. AS WITH THE LONGSTANDING PROHIBITION AGAINST WOMEN ENTERING THE PRIESTHOOD, THERE IS NO FIRM THEOLOGICAL FOUNDATION TO SUPPORT THE TRADITION THAT PRIESTS SHOULD NOT BE ALLOWED TO MARRY.

IN HIS FIRST LETTER TO THE CORINTHIANS
(7:25-40), SAINT PAUL ALLOWED THAT THERE
IS "NO COMMAND FROM THE LORD" ON THE
MATTER EVEN AS HE RECOMMENDED
CELIBACY AS HAVING WORKED WELL FOR HIM.

JOHN PAUL II RECOGNIZED THAT CELIBACY
WAS MERELY BASED ON TRADITION, NOT
SCRIPTURE, AND THAT THERE HAD BEEN
MARRIED CATHOLIC PRIESTS FOR CENTURIES.
BUT HE NONETHELESS MADE IT CLEAR THAT
THE VATICAN WOULD CONTINUE TO DEMAND
THAT PRIESTS BE CELIBATE.

THEN AGAIN, SOME EXPERTS COUNTER THAT CELIBACY DOESN'T EXPLAIN PEDOPHILIA. DENIED SEX, MOST PEOPLE TURN TO CONSENTING ADULTS, NOT CHILDREN.

MORE PERPLEXING, THE RATE OF CATHOLIC PRIESTS WHO SEXUALLY ABUSE CHILDREN DOESN'T SEEM TO BE ANY HIGHER THAN FOR SEXUAL ABUSERS OF CHILDREN IN THE GENERAL POPULATION. SOME EVEN CITE A LOWER RATE (4 PERCENT) FOR CHURCH-RELATED SEXUAL ABUSE OF CHILDREN THAN FOR CHILDHOOD SEXUAL ABUSE OVERALL IN AMERICA (15-20 PERCENT).

IN OTHER WORDS, THE PROBLEM MAY NOT BE
THAT CATHOLICISM OR ITS PRACTICES (LIKE
CELIBACY) CAUSE PEDOPHILIA. INSTEAD,
PEDOPHILIA SEEMS TO EXIST IN ANY LARGE
POPULATION OF PEOPLE.

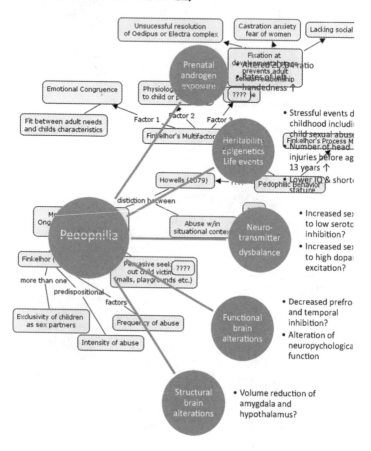

GIVEN THE INFLEXIBLE WAY THAT HE
APPROACHED THE CHALLENGES OF
FEMALE PRIESTS (PERMITTED BY THE
EPISCOPAL CHURCH SINCE 1974), THE
WIDESPREAD USE OF CONTRACEPTION,
AND THE PEDOPHILES UNDER HIS
WATCH, JOHN PAUL'S PAPACY LOOKED
LESS LIKE A MODERN PAPACY THAN A
WHOLESALE ROLLBACK OF VATICAN II.

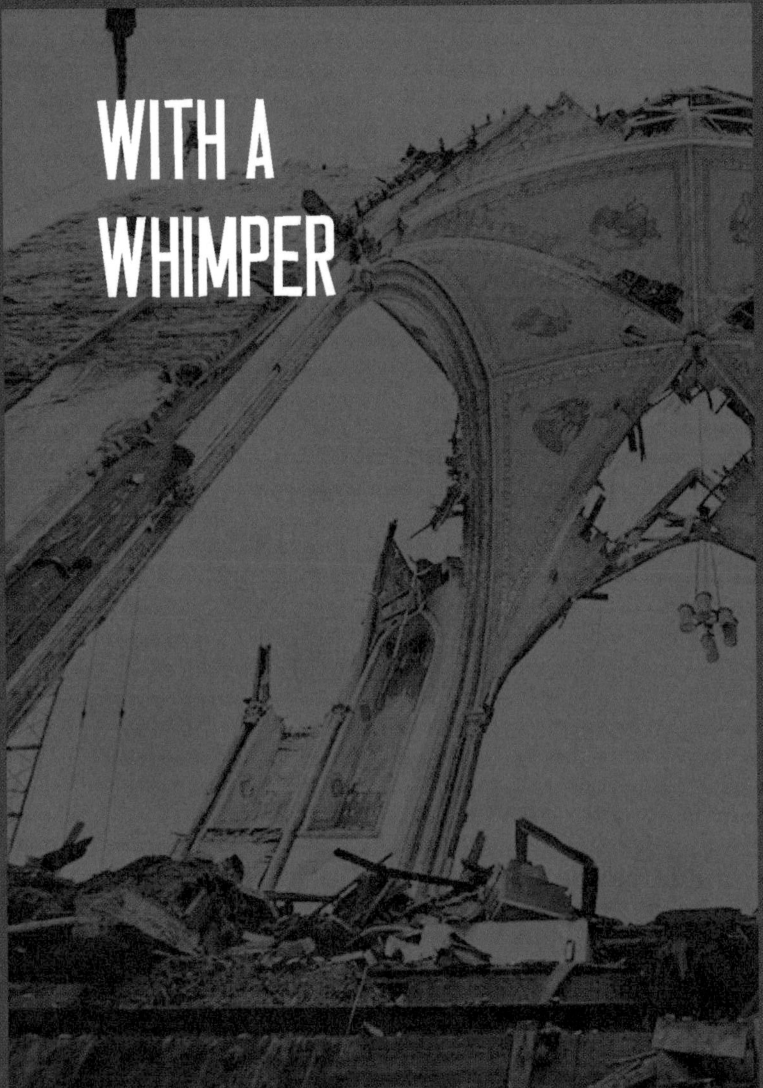
WITH A
WHIMPER

POLITICALLY, THE TURN OF THE TWENTY-FIRST CENTURY IS DEFINED BY THE CONFLICT BETWEEN THE WEST AND RADICAL ISLAMISM.

1998: AL-QAEDA BOMBS US EMBASSIES IN TANZANIA AND KENYA

2000: AL-QAEDA BOMBS USS *COLE* IN YEMEN

2000: US AND JORDANIAN AUTHORITIES FOIL AL-QAEDA "MILLENNIUM PLOT" TO BLOW UP TOURIST SITES, A SHIP, AND AN AIRPORT ON NEW YEAR'S DAY

2001: SEPTEMBER 11 ATTACKS AGAINST NEW YORK AND WASHINGTON, DC

2001: US INVADES AFGHANISTAN (WAR ONGOING)

2003: US INVADES IRAQ (WAR ONGOING)

2009: US ESCALATES USE OF DRONES TO KILL THOUSANDS IN PAKISTAN, SOMALIA, YEMEN, ETC.

2011: US HELPS OVERTHROW GOVERNMENT OF LIBYA, SPARKING A SECOND CIVIL WAR (ONGOING)

2011: US ARMS ISLAMIST REBELS IN SYRIA, CONTRIBUTING TO THE CIVIL WAR (ONGOING)

AMERICA'S BRASH, YOUNG NEW PRESIDENT, GEORGE W. BUSH, RESPONDS TO 9/11 BY TURNING HARD RIGHT. IN RHETORIC REMINISCENT OF THE PAPAL ATTACKS AGAINST MUSLIMS DURING THE MIDDLE AGES, HE DECLARES HIS "CRUSADE" A PERPETUAL GLOBAL "WAR ON TERROR." OTHERS CALL IT "THE FOREVER WAR" AND "THE GREAT WAR FOR CIVILISATION."

THE POLITICAL DEBATE OVER THIS CLASH CREATES A VAST CHASM BETWEEN ANTI-INTERVENTIONIST PROGRESSIVES AND MILITARIST CONSERVATIVES, AND A SPIRITUAL CRISIS FOR THE PEOPLE IN WESTERN SOCIETIES WHO HAD NOT CONDONED TARGETED DRONE ASSASSINATIONS OR BOMBING OF CIVILIANS THIS OPENLY BEFORE.

NOT SHYING AWAY FROM RADICAL ACTIONS,
BUSH ATTACKS AFGHANISTAN AND IRAQ.
OVERSEEING A DEGRADATION OF AMERICA'S
MORAL STANDING, BUSH PERSONALLY
AUTHORIZES THE DETAINMENT OF TERRORISM
SUSPECTS IN SECRET PRISONS. HE GREEN-
LIGHTS POLITICAL ASSASSINATIONS. HE EVEN
ALLOWS PRISON CAMPS WHERE PEOPLE,
INCLUDING CHILDREN, KIDNAPPED FROM
OCCUPIED NATIONS LIKE AFGHANISTAN ARE
INCARCERATED INDEFINITELY, ISOLATED FROM
THEIR FAMILIES, AND DENIED LEGAL
REPRESENTATION AND A FAIR TRIAL.

MEANWHILE, ROMAN CATHOLICISM IS POLITICALLY ADRIFT. AGING AND MORE CONSERVATIVE THAN EVER, JOHN PAUL II'S MORAL VOICE IS RARELY HEARD ON THE WORLD STAGE DURING THIS CRUCIAL PERIOD OF MORAL AMBIGUITY. THE POPE CRITICIZES THE INVASION OF IRAQ AND THE US ABUSE OF IRAQI PRISONERS AT ABU GHRAIB.

WAR CANNOT BE DECIDED UPON, EVEN WHEN IT IS A MATTER OF ENSURING THE COMMON GOOD, EXCEPT AS THE VERY LAST OPTION, AND IN ACCORDANCE WITH VERY STRICT CONDITIONS...

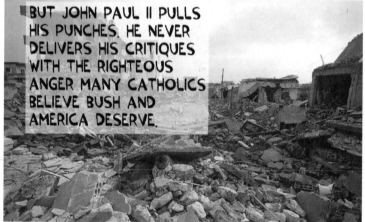

BUT JOHN PAUL II PULLS HIS PUNCHES. HE NEVER DELIVERS HIS CRITIQUES WITH THE RIGHTEOUS ANGER MANY CATHOLICS BELIEVE BUSH AND AMERICA DESERVE.

IS THE POPE'S INNATE CONSERVATISM
RESPONSIBLE FOR HIS FAILURE TO SPEAK
OUT AGAINST BUSH'S ILLEGAL WARS AND
GROTESQUE HUMAN RIGHTS VIOLATIONS?
PERHAPS. THE PONTIFF HAS LOST HIS VIGOR.
HE IS IN HIS EIGHTIES. HE HAS NEVER FULLY
RECOVERED FROM FOUR BULLET WOUNDS
SUSTAINED IN 1981 (IN AN ASSASSINATION
ATTEMPT BY A FAR-RIGHT TURKISH MUSLIM).

WHATEVER THE CAUSE, THE CHURCH'S MORAL
AUTHORITY IS PROFOUNDLY DAMAGED
DURING THE BUSH YEARS.

FINALLY, IN APRIL 2005 THE EIGHTY-FOUR-
YEAR-OLD PONTIFF SUCCUMBS TO HIS
YEARS-LONG BATTLE WITH PARKINSON'S
DISEASE AND OTHER AILMENTS.

HIS DYING WORDS: "LET ME GO TO THE
HOUSE OF THE FATHER."

THE CHURCH HE LEAVES BEHIND HAS ALL BUT
ABOLISHED THE INFLUENCE OF LIBERATION
THEOLOGY. HE HAS STACKED THE RANKS OF
BISHOPS AND CARDINALS WITH
PERSONALITIES WHO ARE DOCTRINALLY
CONSERVATIVE AND ADMINISTRATIVELY LAX.

Catholic Church's Costs Pass $1 Billion in Abuse Cases

Catholic Church withers in Europe

Catholics In Crisis

Why the strength of the Catholic Church now lies in its weakness

A People Adrift: The Crisis of the Roman Catholic Church in

IN SPITE OF HIS PUBLIC PRONOUNCEMENTS OF WORRY, HE FAILED TO CONFRONT THE ROOTS AND CONSEQUENCES OF THE PEDO-PHILIC SCANDALS. UNDER HIS REIGN, [THE SECRET SOCIETY] OPUS DEI GOT STRONGER THAN EVER... THIS IS WHY JOHN PAUL II WAS AN ETHICAL FAILURE — PROOF THAT EVEN A SINCERE, RADICAL ETHICAL STANCE CAN BECOME A FAKE, EMPTY POSE IF IT DOES NOT TAKE INTO ACCOUNT ITS OWN CONDITIONS AND CONSEQUENCES.

Slajov Žižek

April 8, 2005

"The winner [of the election for the next pope] seems certain to continue John Paul II's progressive policies on social issues such as war and peace, human rights and concern for the poor. But on hot-button concerns that so captivate U.S. Catholics, and often the media, expect no changes. That includes the late pope's firm policies against women priests, divorce and remarriage, birth control, gay sex, same-sex marriage, abortion, mercy-killing and stem cell research using human embryos."

—*Associated Press, April 10, 2005*

INDEED, FACED WITH THE OPPORTUNITY TO MODERNIZE THE CHURCH, THE PAPAL CONCLAVE FOLLOWING JOHN PAUL'S DEATH INSTEAD CHOOSES THE SEVENTY-EIGHT-YEAR-OLD JOSEPH RATZINGER OF GERMANY -- A THEOLOGICAL AND POLITICAL CONSERVATIVE, DEAN OF THE COLLEGE OF CARDINALS, AND ONE OF JOHN PAUL'S CLOSEST CONFIDANTS.

POPE BENEDICT XVI, 2005—2013

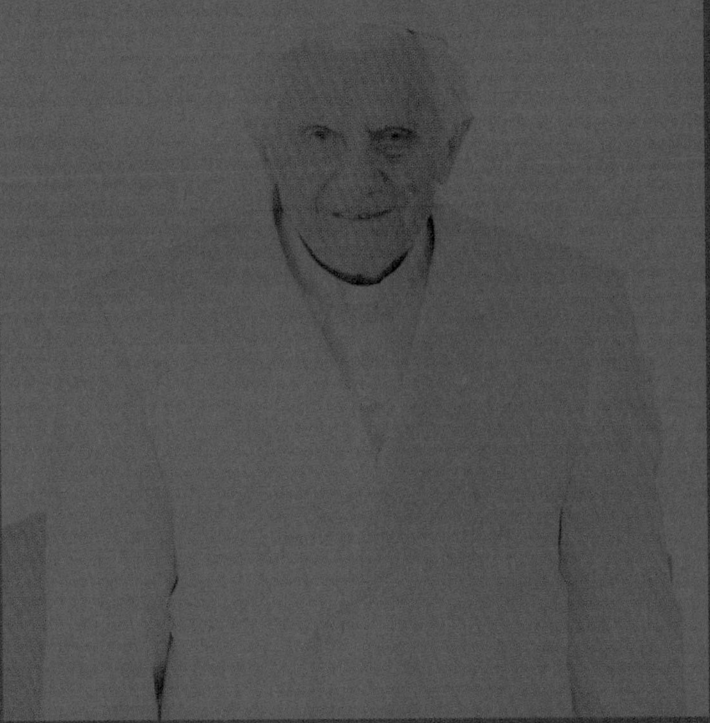

EYEBROWS ARE RAISED WHEN IT SURFACES
THAT RATZINGER WAS CONSCRIPTED INTO
THE HITLER YOUTH AS A BOY.

"NAZI POPE" JIBES AREN'T FAIR: NEITHER HE,
HIS FATHER, NOR ANY MEMBER OF HIS
FAMILY JOINED THE NAZI PARTY. TO THE
CONTRARY, HIS FATHER'S ANTI-NAZI RANTS
FORCED THEM TO GO ON THE RUN SEVERAL
TIMES.

STILL, THE MERE FACT OF HIM BEING OLD
ENOUGH TO HAVE TO EXPLAIN WHAT HE DID
DURING WORLD WAR II MAKES HIM SEEM LIKE
A RELIC, NOT RELEVANT TO A NEW
MILLENNIUM.

DUE TO HIS ADVANCED AGE, VATICAN WATCHERS EXPECT BENEDICT TO BE MORE OF A TRANSITIONAL FIGURE THAN A TRANSFORMATIONAL ONE. A DECADE LATER, BENEDICT RECALLS THAT HE FELT THE SAME WAY:

I DID THINK THAT I MIGHT NOT HAVE THAT MUCH STRENGTH. I COULD NOT START ANY LONG-TERM THINGS.

IN A SHOCKING AND NEARLY UNPRECEDENTED MOVE, BENEDICT ABDICATES AND RETIRES AFTER EIGHT YEARS, AT AGE EIGHTY-SIX.

FEBRUARY 11, 2013: POPE BENEDICT BECOMES THE FIRST POPE TO RESIGN SINCE THE MIDDLE AGES.

THE POPE TOOK A SHEET OF PAPER AND READ FROM IT. HE JUST SAID HE WAS **RESIGNING** AND THAT HE WOULD BE FINISHING ON FEB. 28.

THE CARDINALS WERE JUST LOOKING AT ONE ANOTHER. THEN THE POPE GOT TO HIS FEET, GAVE HIS BENEDICTION AND LEFT.

Monsignor Dr. Oscar Sánchez of Mexico

ACCORDING TO PUBLISHED REPORTS, THE LAST STRAW WAS BENEDICT'S DREAD OF A SCHEDULED TRIP TO RIO DE JANEIRO.

BENEDICT'S BRIEF PAPACY LEAVES THE
CHURCH EVEN WEAKER THAN WHEN HE TOOK
OVER AFTER JOHN PAUL.

"Might be smarter to take a thumb drive
down to the cybercafé."

HIS REACTIONS TO THE CHURCH CULTURE
THAT CONTRIBUTED TO THE CHILD
PEDOPHILIA SCANDAL WERE INCREMENTALIST,
SUCH AS MAKING IT A CHURCH CRIME TO
DOWNLOAD PORNOGRAPHY AND INCREASING
THE STATUTE OF LIMITATIONS FOR CHURCH
PROSECUTION OF A PRIEST FROM TEN TO
TWENTY YEARS.

FURIOUS VICTIMS' ADVOCATES EVEN SAY THEY STILL WANT TO PROSECUTE HIM PERSONALLY FOR HIS INACTION.

[BENEDICT] HAS READ THOUSANDS OF PAGES OF REPORTS OF THE ABUSE CASES FROM ACROSS THE WORLD. HE KNOWS MORE ABOUT CLERGY SEX CRIMES AND COVER-UPS THAN ANYONE ELSE IN THE CHURCH YET HE HAS DONE PRECIOUS LITTLE TO PROTECT CHILDREN.

David Clohessy, executive director of SNAP (Survivors Network of those Abused by Priests)

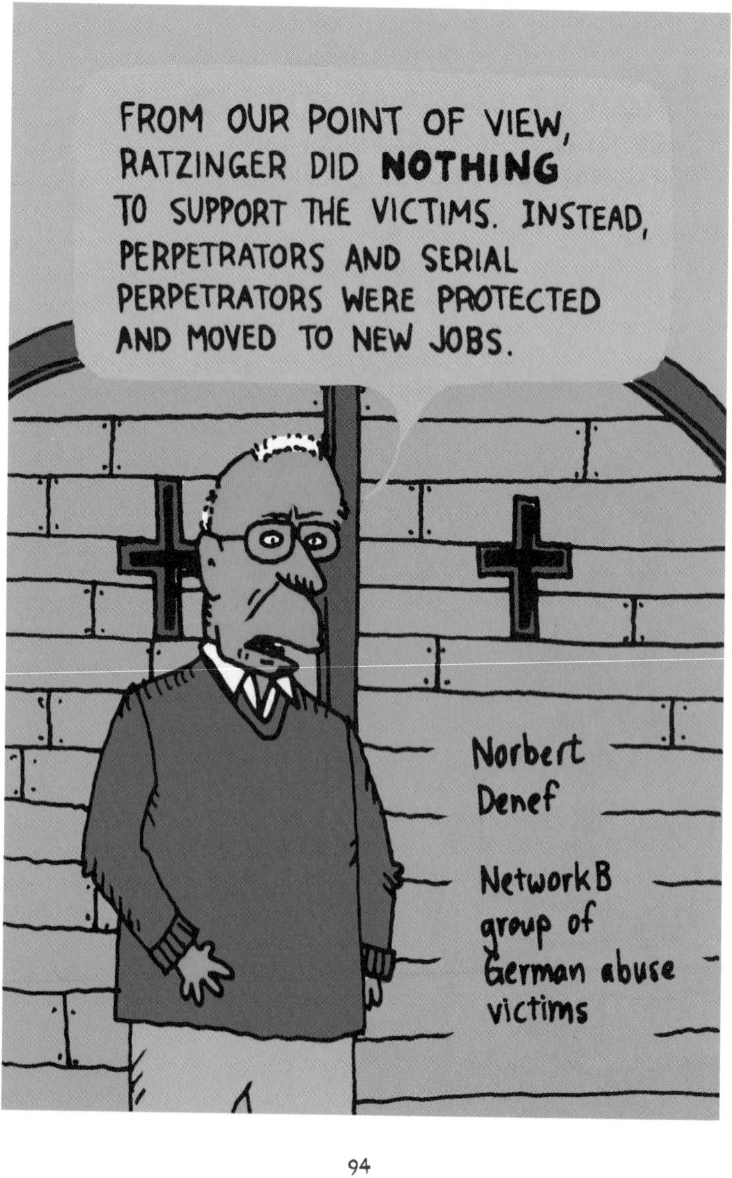
FROM OUR POINT OF VIEW, RATZINGER DID **NOTHING** TO SUPPORT THE VICTIMS. INSTEAD, PERPETRATORS AND SERIAL PERPETRATORS WERE PROTECTED AND MOVED TO NEW JOBS.
Norbert Denef
NetworkB group of German abuse victims

THE CATHOLIC CHURCH IS A MESS.

THE PROBLEMS FACING THE CHURCH REMAIN: THE CHILD ABUSE SCANDAL HAS NOT BEEN RESOLVED, NOR HAS THE CHURCH'S LOSS OF AUTHORITY AND SELF-CONFIDENCE BEEN REVERSED.

IN THE WEST, AND EUROPE WAS CLEARLY THE FOCUS OF BENEDICT'S INTEREST, THE DECLINE IN CHURCH ATTENDANCES AND THE LACK OF VOCATIONS TO STAFF THE FUTURE PRIESTHOOD, THE SHEER DISINTEGRATION IN ITS STATUS AND ESTEEM, HAVE BEEN NEITHER CONFRONTED NOR RESOLVED.

Stephen Bates
The Guardian
Feb. 11. 2013

Michael Walsh, British papal historian

STUDENTS OF CATHOLICISM ARE IN A DEEP FUNK BECAUSE BENEDICT CONTINUES TO PURGE PROGRESSIVE VOICES FROM THE RANKS OF THE TOP LEADERSHIP IN ROME, FROM WHICH THE NEXT POPE WILL BE CHOSEN.

DURING [BENEDICT'S] TIME IN OFFICE, HE HAS ORDAINED SO MANY CONSERVATIVE CARDINALS, THAT AMONGST THEM IS HARDLY A SINGLE PERSON TO BE FOUND WHO COULD LEAD THE CHURCH OUT OF ITS MULTIFACETED CRISIS.

Hans Küng
Swiss theologian
Feb. 11, 2013

CORPORATE STRATEGISTS ADVISE THEIR CLIENTS: UNDERPROMISE AND OVERDELIVER.

EXPECTATIONS FOR THE POST-BENEDICT PAPACY COULDN'T HAVE BEEN LOWER.

AND THE CHANGE OF DIRECTION COULDN'T HAVE BEEN MORE DRAMATIC.

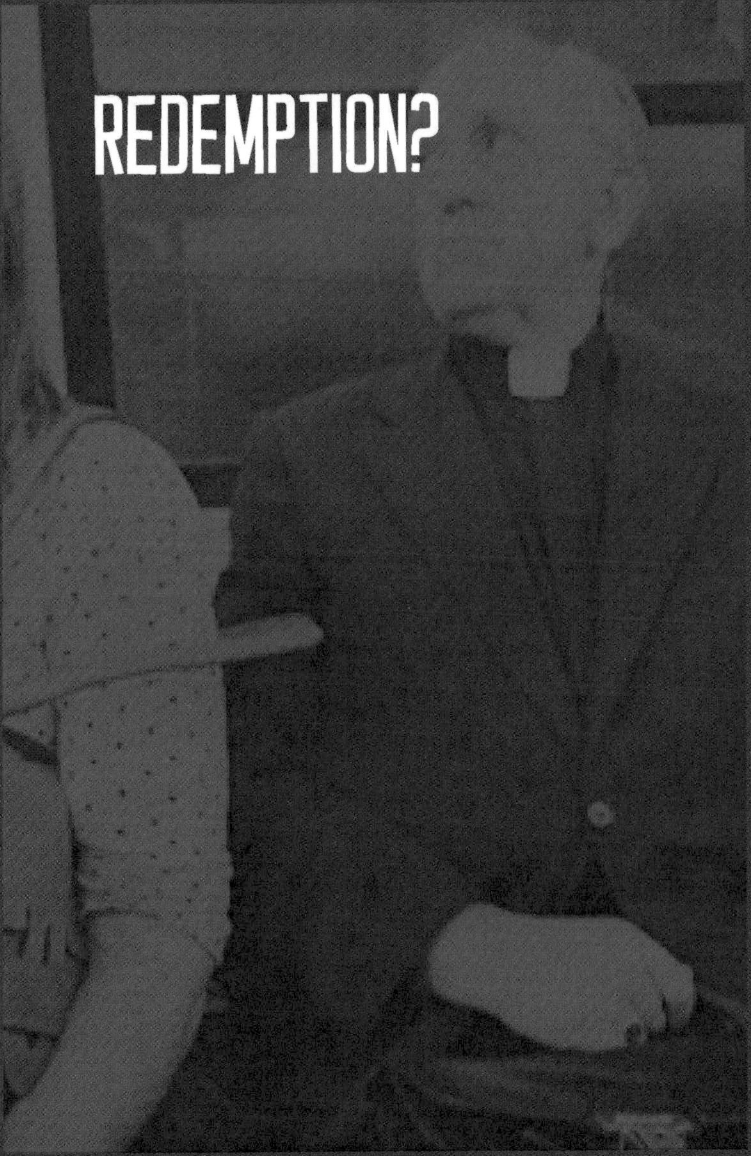
REDEMPTION?

MEMBERS OF THE 2013 ELECTORAL
CONCLAVE RESPONSIBLE FOR ELECTING THE
POPE RECALL THAT DURING PRELIMINARY
DISCUSSIONS THE NAME OF CARDINAL
JORGE BERGOGLIO OF ARGENTINA DIDN'T
COME UP AT FIRST.

ALSO, AT SEVENTY-SIX -- ESPECIALLY IN
LIGHT OF BENEDICT'S SURPRISE
RESIGNATION -- SOME CHURCH OBSERVERS
THINK BERGOGLIO IS TOO OLD.

TRUE, BERGOGLIO WAS A RUNNER-UP IN THE
CONCLAVE THAT SELECTED BENEDICT IN
2005. BUT TRADITION DICTATES THAT
HAVING COME CLOSE BEFORE IS USUALLY
HELD AGAINST A CANDIDATE.

THE 2013 CONCLAVE IS DEFINED BY A RIFT
BETWEEN TWO CAMPS: THE "ROMAN" AND
THE "REFORM."

THE FORMER ARE TRADITIONALISTS
LOOKING TO DEFEND THE PAPAL
BUREAUCRACY, WHILE THE LATTER ARE
PUSHING FOR DECISIVE INSTITUTIONAL
CHANGE.

THE BACKDROP IS YET ANOTHER SCANDAL.
[DURING THE MID-19TH CENTURY, THE CATHOLIC CHURCH] HAD 15,000 SQUARE MILES OF WHAT WAS CENTRAL ITALY WITH THOUSANDS OF SUBJECTS. THEY LEVIED TAXES AND PAID FOR THIS LAVISH LIFESTYLE – WITH 700 SERVANTS AND A BIG AND GROWING BUREAUCRACY AROUND THEM. THEN, IN 1870, ITALY'S NATIONALISTS HAVE A REVOLUTION. THEY THROW THE POPE OUT, THEY GET RID OF THE PAPAL STATES. THE VATICAN GOES FROM BEING AN EMPIRE – TO A LITTLE POSTAGE-STAMP SIZE OF PROPERTY CALLED VATICAN CITY.
Gerald Posner
author of God's Bankers

BY WORLD WAR II, THE CATHOLIC CHURCH WAS INVOLVED IN FINANCIAL TRANSACTIONS -- SOME ABOVE BOARD, OTHERS NOT SO MUCH.

LEADERS CREATED THE VATICAN BANK (FORMAL NAME: "INSTITUTE FOR THE WORKS OF RELIGION") IN ORDER TO CONDUCT BUSINESS WITH GERMAN COMPANIES FREE FROM THE SCRUTINY OF THE ALLIES.

THEY BUNDLED TOGETHER LIFE INSURANCE POLICIES OF JEWISH REFUGEES WHO HAD BEEN SENT TO AUSCHWITZ AND OTHER DEATH CAMPS. THEY ESCHEATED THESE POLICIES EARLY ON— MEANING THEY TOOK THE CASH VALUE OF THEM. [WHEN CHILDREN OR GRANDCHILDREN OF HOLOCAUST VICTIMS TRIED TO COLLECT ON THE POLICIES,] THESE INSURANCE COMPANIES WOULD REFUSE TO PAY OUT[,] SAYING: "SHOW US A DEATH CERTIFICATE," WHICH THEY KNEW WAS IMPOSSIBLE. THEY WOULD KEEP THE MONEY.

[THE VATICAN BANK IS] ESSENTIALLY AN OFFSHORE BANK IN THE MIDDLE OF A FOREIGN COUNTRY — SO THAT ONCE THAT BANK WAS FORMED, IT MEANT THAT SOMEBODY SITTING OVER IN ITALY WHO HAD A LOT OF MONEY, ALL THEY HAD TO DO WAS FIND A PRIEST OR CLERIC INSIDE VATICAN CITY TO TAKE THEIR MONEY IN SUITCASES OF CASH ACROSS THE STREET — JUST WAIT FOR THE RED LIGHT TO TURN GREEN — WALK IT OVER ON A CART, DEPOSIT IT IN THE VATICAN BANK, AND IT NO LONGER COULD BE TAXED. IT NO LONGER COULD BE FOLLOWED BY ITALIAN AUTHORITIES. IT COULDN'T BE FOLLOWED FOR A DRUG INVESTIGATION. SO WHAT DOES THAT RESULT IN? IT RESULTS IN THE VATICAN BANK BEING ONE OF THE TOP BANKS IN THE WORLD FOR MONEY LAUNDERING — A HAVEN OFTEN FOR THESE BUSINESS EXECUTIVES INVOLVED IN SCANDALS IN ITALY.

ON JUNE 28, 2013, ITALIAN POLICE ARREST A PRIEST AND VATICAN BANK OFFICIAL, MONSIGNOR NUNZIO SCARANO.

The Telegraph

Spy, monsignor and banker arrested in Vatican bank fraud 'plot'

An Italian spy, a Vatican official and banker have been arrested on suspicion of corruption and fraud involving an alleged plot to bring 20 million euros in cash into Italy from Switzerland aboard a government plane.

Monsignor Nunzio Scarano

VOA

Arrested Vatican Prelate Lived Lush Life in Hometown

BUSINESS DAY

Of Virtue and Vice, and a Vatican Priest

Some See Msgr. Nunzio Scarano, Who Is Accused of Money Laundering, As a Symbol of a Financial System Gone Awry

"MONSIGNOR CINQUECENTO," WHO EARNS HIS NICKNAME FROM THE €500 BILLS HE CARRIES, IS ACCUSED OF TRYING TO SMUGGLE €20 MILLION BY PRIVATE PLANE FROM SWITZERLAND TO MAFIA-CONNECTED BUSINESSMEN IN THE NAPLES REGION.

nzio
69

Luis Antonio
Tagle, 55
Philippines

Jean-Louis
Tauran, 69
France (Curia)

Julio
Terrazas Sandoval, 76
Bolivia

Dionigi
Tettamanzi, 78
Italy

Baselios Cleemis
Thottunkal, 53
India

ude
, 76
ia

Raúl
Vela Chiriboga, 79
Ecuador

IN THE EMBARRASSING WAKE OF THE VATICAN BANK CORRUPTION AND PEDOPHILE COVER-UP SCANDALS, REFORMISTS IN THE CONCLAVE GAIN POWER AND INFLUENCE. THEY WANT A POPE WHO WILL CLEAN UP THE ROMAN CURIA, THE VATICAN BUREAUCRACY.

THEY ARE DRAWN TO FIGURES WHO REFLECT THE CHURCH'S DEMOGRAPHIC SHIFT TOWARD LATIN AMERICA, WHERE THE CHURCH IS STILL GROWING.

Cruz
, 77
al

Giovanni Battista
Re, 79
Italy

o
ra, 70

Francisco
Robles Ortega, 63
Mexico

Franc
Rode, 78
Slovenia

Oscar
Rodriguez Maradiaga, 70
Honduras

Paolo
Romeo, 75
Italy

Antonio Maria
Rouco Varela, 76
Spain

Leonardo

Robert

Paolo

Theodore-Adrien

Odlin Paden

THE TRADITIONALIST "ROMANS" IN THE
CONCLAVE PREFER AN ITALIAN, OR AT
LEAST A EUROPEAN, WHO WILL LEAVE
THINGS PRETTY MUCH AS THEY ARE.

THAT SAID, ONCE THE PROCEEDINGS ARE UNDERWAY, BERGOGLIO EMERGES AS A STRONG CONTENDER QUICKLY. AT NO TIME IS HE EVER COMPLETELY OUTSIDE OF THE RUNNING.

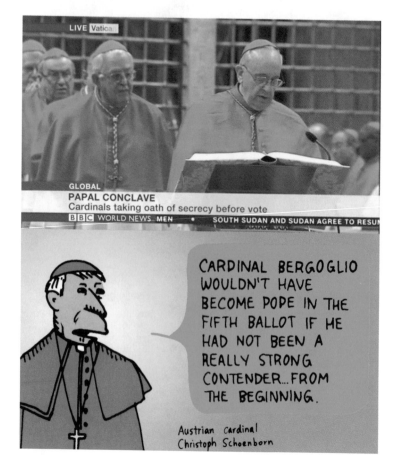

LIVE Vatica

GLOBAL
PAPAL CONCLAVE
Cardinals taking oath of secrecy before vote
BBC WORLD NEWS MEN • SOUTH SUDAN AND SUDAN AGREE TO RESUM

CARDINAL BERGOGLIO WOULDN'T HAVE BECOME POPE IN THE FIFTH BALLOT IF HE HAD NOT BEEN A REALLY STRONG CONTENDER...FROM THE BEGINNING.

Austrian cardinal
Christoph Schoenborn

SOME OF THE "ROMAN" CONTINGENT LIKE THAT HE IS ETHNICALLY ITALIAN, WITH TWO ITALIAN-BORN PARENTS.

HE IS NOT PART OF THE ITALIAN SYSTEM, BUT... BECAUSE OF HIS CULTURE AND BACKGROUND, HE WAS **ITALO-COM-PATIBLE**.

IF THERE WAS A CHANCE THAT SOMEONE COULD INTERVENE WITH JUSTICE IN [REFORMING THE CURIA] HE WAS THE MAN WHO COULD DO IT BEST.

French cardinal
André Vingt-Trois

BERGOGLIO IS VIEWED AS CONSERVATIVE ON SOCIAL ISSUES WITHIN THE CHURCH. BUT THE SYMBOLISM OF THE FIRST LATIN AMERICAN PONTIFF IN TWO THOUSAND YEARS HITS AN IDENTITY-POLITICS SWEET SPOT. HE IS A NATURAL COMPROMISE.

I THINK IT ALL CAME TOGETHER IN AN EXTRAORDINARY FASHION. YOU DON'T ASK WHY [THE ROMAN FACTION] CHANGED THEIR VOTES. NOR DO YOU KNOW WHO CHANGED THEIR VOTES. BUT IT BECAME FAIRLY CLEAR AS WE VOTED THAT PERHAPS IT WAS GOING TO GO IN SOME OTHER UNEXPECTED WAY, BUT MORE QUICKLY ALSO. THERE ARE SURPRISES. THAT'S A SIGN OF THE HOLY SPIRIT, I THINK.

Chicago cardinal Francis George, 1937-2015

LITTLE DOES THE ROMAN FACTION REALIZE HOW MUCH THINGS ARE ABOUT TO CHANGE.

THE REVOLUTION
WILL BE PAPALIZED

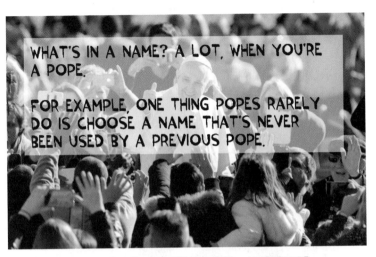

WHAT'S IN A NAME? A LOT, WHEN YOU'RE A POPE.

FOR EXAMPLE, ONE THING POPES RARELY DO IS CHOOSE A NAME THAT'S NEVER BEEN USED BY A PREVIOUS POPE.

MARCH 16, 2013: FIRST PAPAL AUDIENCE WITH MEDIA...SPEAKING TO REPORTERS ABOUT HOW HE CHOSE HIS NAME WITH HELP FROM HIS FRIEND, BRAZILIAN CARDINAL CLAUDIO HUMMES:

[HUMMES] EMBRACED ME AND KISSED ME AND SAID: "DON'T FORGET THE POOR"... AND THAT STRUCK ME... THE POOR... IMMEDIATELY I THOUGHT OF SAINT FRANCIS OF ASSISI. FRANCIS WAS A MAN OF PEACE, A MAN OF POVERTY, A MAN WHO LOVED AND PROTECTED CREATION...

THROUGHOUT HIS CAREER, CARDINAL
BERGOGLIO CULTIVATED A REPUTATION AS
DOCTRINALLY CONSERVATIVE, PERSONALLY
HUMBLE, AND DEEPLY VESTED IN THE
PROBLEMS OF THE POOR. WHICH OF THESE
ASPECTS WILL HE EMPHASIZE FIRST?

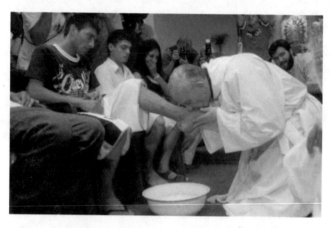

WELL AWARE THAT HIS EARLY ACTIONS AS
PONTIFF WILL BE SCRUTINIZED, HE VISITS A
JUVENILE DETENTION CENTER IN ROME, THE
CASAL DEL MARMO. EVOKING THE FAMOUS
PASSAGE FROM JOHN 13:1-17 IN WHICH JESUS
WASHES HIS DISCIPLES' FEET, POPE FRANCIS
TELLS TEN MALE AND TWO FEMALE
PRISONERS THAT HE IS AT THEIR SERVICE,
AND WASHES AND KISSES THEIR FEET. TWO
ARE MUSLIM.

FRANCIS'S "CONSERVATISM" DIFFERS FROM
THAT OF HIS PREDECESSORS. HE WANTS THE
WORLD TO KNOW THAT RIGHT AWAY.

Vatican Ends Battle With U.S. Catholic Nuns' Group

**Under Pope Francis,
Vatican changes its
tone toward American
nuns**

Pope orders study of women's role in
early Church, cheering equality
campaigners

POPE BENEDICT XVI HAD ORDERED AN
INVESTIGATION INTO THE US LEADERSHIP
CONFERENCE OF WOMEN RELIGIOUS, A NUNS'
GROUP THE VATICAN BELIEVED HAD MOVED
TOO FAR TO THE LEFT WITH ITS INTERESTS
IN FEMINISM AND SOCIAL JUSTICE. LIBERALS
WERE UPSET BY THIS CHILLING OF FEMALE
ACTIVISM WITHIN THE CHURCH. UPON TAKING
OFFICE, POPE FRANCIS ORDERS THAT THE
INVESTIGATION WRAP UP ITS WORK. THE
INQUIRY CONCLUDES WITH THE VATICAN'S
EFFUSIVE PRAISE FOR THE NUNS' EFFORTS.

EAGER TO MAKE HIS MARK AS A REFORMER, FRANCIS MOVES QUICKLY TO CLEAN UP THE SCANDAL-SCARRED VATICAN BANK. A FEW MONTHS INTO HIS PAPACY, THE BANK ISSUES ITS FIRST-EVER ANNUAL REPORT, PART OF FRANCIS'S PUSH TO IMPROVE THE BANK'S TRANSPARENCY.

THE NEW POPE HIRES AN INDEPENDENT CONSULTING FIRM TO AUDIT THE BANK'S BOOKS, REPLACES FOUR OF THE FIVE CARDINALS OVERSEEING THE BANK, AND ASSIGNS OUTSIDE EXPERTS TO SUPERVISE ITS OPERATIONS.

TWO YEARS LATER, IN 2015:

THE BANK HAS GONE FROM THE SHADOWS TO THE REALM OF MAINSTREAM BANKING. THEY ENDED THE ANONYMOUS NUMBERED ACCOUNTS, AND THEY INSTITUTED "KNOW YOUR CUSTOMER" RULES.

Professor Martijn Cremers, finance dept. University of Notre Dame

IN WHAT WOULD BECOME THE DEFINING QUOTE OF HIS NEW PAPACY, FRANCIS ANSWERS A REPORTER'S QUESTION ABOUT HIS VIEWS ON PRIESTS DISCOVERED TO BE GAY:

THIS MARKS A RADICAL DEPARTURE FROM THE TONE OF HIS PREDECESSORS, IF NOT NECESSARILY FROM THEIR POLICY.

POPE BENEDICT, IN 2005, WAS STILL CITING A DOCUMENT FROM 1986: HOMOSEXUALITY IS A "STRONG TENDENCY ORDERED TOWARD AN INTRINSIC MORAL EVIL" AND AN "OBJECTIVE DISORDER."

FRANCIS DOESN'T EXPLICITLY ENDORSE HOMOSEXUALITY OR STATE THAT IT'S ACCEPTABLE WITHIN THE CHURCH. YET HE MAKES NEWS BY DISCUSSING THE SUBJECT WITH KINDNESS.

IT IS AN OLIVE BRANCH TO GAYS, AS WELL AS TO LIBERAL MEMBERS OF THE LAITY.

AT A CERTAIN POINT, TONE BECOMES SUBSTANCE IF IT'S SEEN AS REVITALIZING THE PROSPECTS OF THE CHURCH... HE'S COMPLETELY CHANGED THE NARRATIVE ABOUT THE CHURCH. IN FIVE MONTHS, NOW THE DOMINANT CATHOLIC STORY IS "CHARISMATIC POPE TAKES WORLD BY STORM."

John L. Allen, Jr., Vatican expert at the *National Catholic Reporter*

SIX MONTHS AFTER TAKING OFFICE,
FRANCIS SHOCKS THE CHURCH BY
EXPOUNDING HIS VIEW THAT THE CHURCH
HAS BECOME TOO HARDLINE AND NEEDS TO
PUT MERCY AHEAD OF DOGMA. IN A
WIDE-RANGING INTERVIEW, HE DECLARES THAT
THE CHURCH HAS GROWN "OBSESSED" WITH
THE ISSUES OF ABORTION, GAY MARRIAGE,
AND CONTRACEPTION, WHICH HAS TURNED
AWAY MORE LIBERAL CATHOLICS. HE STILL
SEEMS TO AGREE WITH CHURCH TEACHINGS
ON THESE ISSUES, BUT HE REFRAINS FROM
MORALIZING.

The New York Times

Pope Says Church Is 'Obsessed' With Gays, Abortion and Birth Control

Riccardo De Luca/Associated Press

Pope Francis' surprising comments came in a lengthy interview in which he criticized the church for putting dogma before love, and for prioritizing moral doctrines over serving the poor and marginalized.

By LAURIE GOODSTEIN
Published: September 19, 2013 | 🗩 1488 Comments

1 Six months into his papacy, Pope Francis sent shock waves through
the Roman Catholic church on Thursday with the publication of his

FRANCIS EXPLAINS THAT THE CHURCH HAS TOO OFTEN PRIORITIZED DOGMA OVER LOVE, AND BEEN PATRONIZING RATHER THAN SERVING THE POOR AND MARGINALIZED.

IT IS NOT NECESSARY TO TALK ABOUT THESE ISSUES ALL THE TIME. THE DOGMATIC AND MORAL TEACHINGS OF THE CHURCH ARE NOT ALL EQUIVALENT. THE CHURCH'S PASTORAL MINISTRY CANNOT BE OBSESSED WITH THE TRANSMISSION OF A DISJOINTED MULTITUDE OF DOCTRINES TO BE IMPOSED INSISTENTLY.

FRANCIS IS THAT RARE EXCEPTIONAL ACTOR WHO CAN CHANGE THE WORLD WITH NUANCE AND TONE. THIS IS A CASE WHERE A MAN'S HARD-EARNED WISDOM AND COURAGE CAN RESTORE THE FAITH OF HUNDREDS OF MILLIONS OF CATHOLICS AND RESTORE SOME KIND OF GOODNESS TO THE WORLD, EVEN WITHOUT CHANGING THE CORE DOGMA OF THE CATHOLIC CHURCH.

WE HAVE TO FIND A NEW BALANCE, OTHERWISE EVEN THE MORAL EDIFICE OF THE CHURCH IS LIKELY TO FALL LIKE A HOUSE OF CARDS, LOSING THE FRESHNESS AND FRAGRANCE OF THE GOSPEL.

PERHAPS THE MOST DECISIVE CHANGE IN TONE IS FOUND IN FRANCIS'S REFRESHINGLY MODERN VIEWS ON SEX.

GOD HIMSELF CREATED SEXUALITY, WHICH IS A MARVELOUS GIFT TO HIS CREATURES... THE STIRRING OF DESIRE OR REPUGNANCE IS NEITHER SINFUL NOR BLAMEWORTHY... HENCE IT CAN NO LONGER SIMPLY BE SAID THAT ALL THOSE IN ANY "IRREGULAR" SITUATION ARE LIVING IN A STATE OF MORTAL SIN.

STILL, TENSIONS REMAIN BETWEEN TRADITIONALISM AND MODERNISM, IN BOTH FRANCIS'S OUTLOOK AND THAT OF HIS CHURCH. IN HIS ENCYCLICAL *AMORIS LÆTITIA* (THE JOY OF LOVE), HE HOLDS TO THE OLD-SCHOOL VIEW THAT TRANSGENDER IDENTITY IS A PERSONAL CHOICE RATHER THAN BIOLOGICALLY HARDWIRED.

HUMAN IDENTITY BECOMES THE CHOICE OF THE INDIVIDUAL, ONE WHICH CAN ALSO CHANGE OVER TIME.

BUT IT'S STILL A BIG DEAL. IN AMERICA AND OTHER WESTERN COUNTRIES, CATHOLICS HAD LARGELY BEEN IGNORING CHURCH DOGMA ABOUT SEX, CONTRACEPTION, AND ABORTION. PEOPLE VIEWED CHURCH OFFICIALS AS LIVING IN THE PAST. BY ACKNOWLEDGING THEIR REALITY, POPE FRANCIS IS TRYING TO CATCH UP TO HIS FLOCK.

THE CHURCH TEACHES THAT LIFE IS A GIFT, SO CONTRACEPTION IS WRONG.

EXCUSE ME, FATHER, BUT YOU **CAN'T** HAVE A FAMILY, RIGHT?

FRANCIS'S CHARM/REFORM OFFENSIVE SHOWS NO SIGN OF PETERING OUT. IN JULY 2014 HE MEETS WITH VICTIMS OF SEXUAL ABUSE BY PEDOPHILE PRIESTS FOR THE FIRST TIME.

BEFORE GOD AND HIS PEOPLE I EXPRESS MY SORROW FOR THE SINS AND **GRAVE CRIMES** OF CLERICAL SEXUAL ABUSE COMMITTED AGAINST YOU. AND I HUMBLY ASK FORGIVENESS. I BEG YOUR FORGIVENESS, TOO, FOR THE SINS OF OMISSION ON THE PART OF CHURCH LEADERS WHO DID NOT RESPOND ADEQUATELY TO REPORTS OF ABUSE MADE BY FAMILY MEMBERS, AS WELL AS BY ABUSE VICTIMS THEMSELVES.

FRANCIS PROMISES TO HOLD ACCOUNTABLE ANY CHURCH OFFICIALS WHO MOLEST CHILDREN, OR WHO DO NOT ADEQUATELY PROTECT CHILDREN FROM THOSE WHO DO.

WE NEED TO DO EVERYTHING IN OUR POWER TO ENSURE THAT THESE SINS HAVE **NO PLACE** IN THE CHURCH.

NOT EVERYONE IS IMPRESSED.

THESE MEETINGS ARE PUBLIC RELATIONS COUPS FOR THE VATICAN AND DISTRACTING PLACEBOS FOR OTHERS. THEY PROVIDE TEMPORARY BUT FALSE HOPE.

Mary Caplan, SNAP
(Survivors Network of those
Abused by Priests)

IN OCTOBER 2014, POPE FRANCIS PRESIDES
OVER A SYNOD OF BISHOPS DEDICATED TO
ISSUES OF FAMILY. AN INTERIM REPORT
MIDWAY THROUGH THE ASSEMBLY STATES
THAT GAYS AND LESBIANS HAVE "GIFTS
AND QUALITIES TO OFFER THE CHRISTIAN
COMMUNITY," BUT BISHOPS ALTER THIS
PHRASING BY THE FINAL REPORT TO NOTE
ONLY THAT HOMOSEXUALS MUST BE
"RECEIVED WITH RESPECT AND GENTLENESS,"
AND THAT "EVERY SIGN OF UNJUST
DISCRIMINATION IN THEIR REGARD SHOULD BE
AVOIDED."

FRANCIS SUPPORTS MOVING TOWARD
LETTING DIVORCED AND REMARRIED
CATHOLICS RECEIVE HOLY COMMUNION, BUT
THIS ALSO IS TOO MUCH TOO SOON FOR
THE SYNOD. THOUGH THE SECTIONS
PERTAINING TO THESE ISSUES FAIL TO
OBTAIN THE REQUIRED TWO-THIRDS
MAJORITY OF VOTES, THEY ARE STILL
INCLUDED IN THE FINAL REPORT -- A MOVE
SOME EXPERTS REGARD AS UNPRECEDENTED.

IN MAY 2017 FRANCIS MAKES ANOTHER OVERTURE TO THE LGBT COMMUNITY, NAMING FATHER JOHN P. DOLAN, PASTOR OF AN AVOWEDLY PRO-LGBT PARISH, AS AUXILIARY BISHOP OF SAN DIEGO.

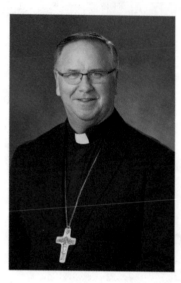

MOST REVEREND
JOHN P. DOLAN

ABIDE IN MY LOVE

ORDAINED: JULY 1, 1989
APPOINTED AUXILIARY BISHOP OF SAN DIEGO: APRIL 19, 2017
CONSECRATED: JUNE 8, 2017

DOLAN'S WAS THE HIGHEST-PROFILE, BUT NOT THE FIRST, PRO-LGBT PROMOTION IN THE US ORCHESTRATED BY POPE FRANCIS.

FRANCIS'S CHARM OFFENSIVE BRANCHES OUT FROM SOCIAL ISSUES TO INCLUDE EVEN THE BASIS OF THE CHURCH ITSELF. PREVIOUS POPES HAVE DISCUSSED THEIR DESIRE TO REVERSE THE GREAT SCHISM OF 1054, WHICH SPLIT THE CATHOLIC CHURCH BASED IN ROME FROM THE EASTERN ORTHODOX CHURCH CENTERED IN CONSTANTINOPLE (NOW ISTANBUL).

BUT IN NOVEMBER 2014 FRANCIS BECOMES THE FIRST TO PROFFER THAT REUNIFICATION COULD OCCUR ON AN EQUAL FOOTING RATHER THAN INSISTING ON ROMAN CATHOLIC DOMINANCE:

"TO REACH THE DESIRED GOAL OF FULL UNITY, THE CATHOLIC CHURCH DOES NOT INTEND TO IMPOSE ANY CONDITIONS EXCEPT THAT OF THE SHARED PROFESSION OF FAITH."

NO DOUBT ABOUT IT: FRANCIS IS A BREATH OF FRESH AIR TO AN INSTITUTION THAT BADLY NEEDS IT.

BUT HE ISN'T A WILD-EYED LIBERATOR. PERHAPS FEELING UNDER SIEGE BY MEDIA COVERAGE THAT BOILS DOWN TO "AWESOME COOL POPE CHANGES UP CHURCH" DAY AFTER DAY, CHURCH CONSERVATIVES DECIDE TO REMIND US THAT FRANCIS IS MORE LIKE THEM ON THE ISSUES THEY CARE ABOUT MOST.

Pope Francis's Radical Authenticity Is Revolutionizing the Catholic Church

8 Ways Pope Francis Is Changing the Direction of the Catholic Church

THE
FRANCIS
EFFECT

JOHN GEHRING

The
FRANCIS
MIRACLE

Inside the Transformation of the Pope and the Church

Shaking Up the Vatican

JOHN L. ALLEN, JR.

POPE FRANCIS

RAYMOND LEO BURKE, A CONSERVATIVE US CARDINAL AND PREFECT OF THE SUPREME TRIBUNAL OF THE APOSTOLIC SIGNATURA, POINTS OUT, IN THE VATICAN NEWSPAPER *L'OSSERVATORE ROMANO*, THAT POPE FRANCIS OPPOSES BOTH ABORTION AND GAY MARRIAGE.

VATICAN SPOKESMAN REVEREND FEDERICO LOMBARDI SAYS THAT POPE FRANCIS DOESN'T PLAN TO CHANGE OR REDEFINE DOGMA ABOUT CHURCH THEOLOGY OR DOCTRINE.

" CONSEQUENCES RELATING TO THE TEACHING OF THE CHURCH ARE NOT TO BE INFERRED FROM THESE OCCURRENCES."

Vatican spokesman
Reverend Federico Lombardi

CATHOLIC POLICY WILL REMAIN LARGELY
THE SAME. WHAT FRANCIS BRINGS IS A MORE
OPEN, MORE WITH-IT TONE, ALONG WITH
GREATER TRANSPARENCY WITHIN THE
CHURCH BUREAUCRACY.

FRANCIS'S CHURCH MIGHT NOT LET
CATHOLICS DO WHAT THEY WANT. BUT
UNLIKE BEFORE, IT WILL LISTEN TO THEM.

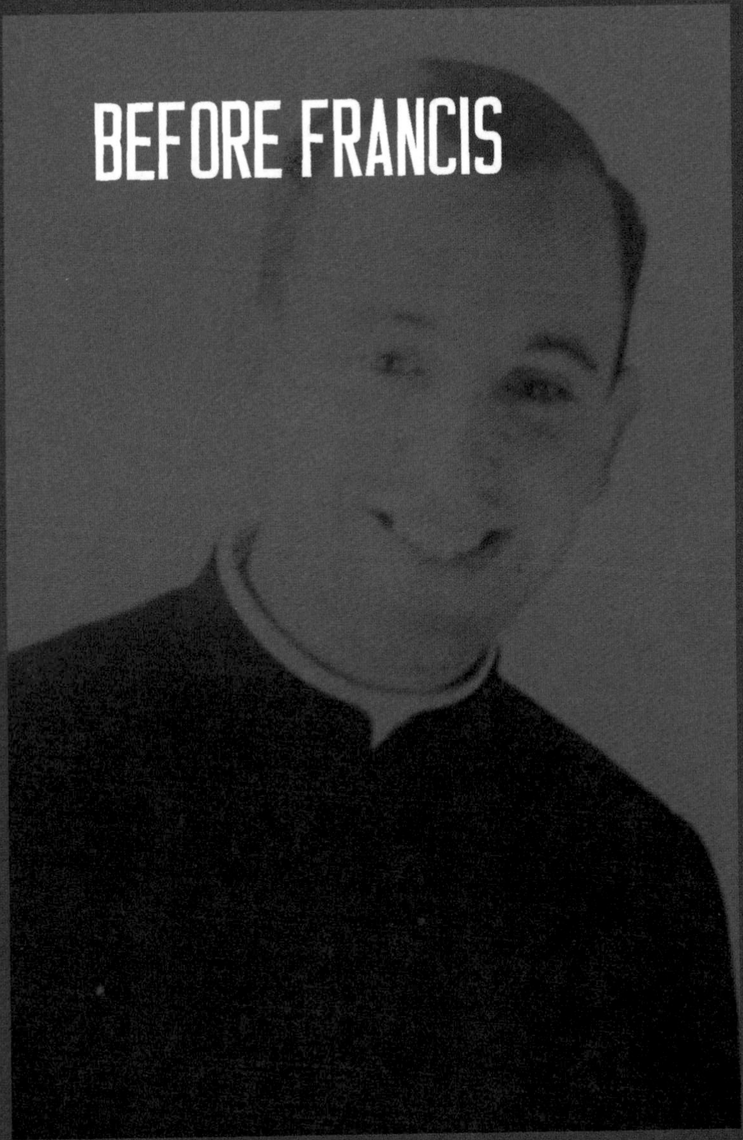
BEFORE FRANCIS

JORGE MARIO BERGOGLIO WAS BORN ON
DECEMBER 17, 1936, IN BUENOS AIRES. HIS
FATHER, MARIO JOSE BERGOGLIO, WAS A
RAILWAY WORKER AND ACCOUNTANT
WHOSE FAMILY IMMIGRATED TO ARGENTINA
FROM ITALY TO ESCAPE THE FASCIST
REGIME OF BENITO MUSSOLINI.

HIS MOTHER, REGINA MARÍA SÍVORI, WAS A
HOUSEWIFE FROM ARGENTINA, ALSO OF
NORTHERN ITALIAN EXTRACTION.

ITALIANS CONSTITUTED THE LARGEST SOURCE OF IMMIGRATION TO ARGENTINA, AND IT'S ESTIMATED THAT UP TO 62.5 PERCENT OF ARGENTINES TODAY HAVE SOME DEGREE OF ITALIAN DESCENT.

BUENOS AIRES WAS A PARTICULARLY IMPORTANT DESTINATION FOR ITALIAN IMMIGRANTS, AND THEY IN TURN HAVE BEEN A MAJOR INFLUENCE IN THE CITY'S CONTINUING CULTURAL SOPHISTICATION AND ECONOMIC AFFLUENCE. THE BERGOGLIOS RAISED THEIR BROOD IN THE MIDDLE-CLASS FLORES BARRIO OF THE ARGENTINE CAPITAL.

BUT THEY WEREN'T MIDDLE-CLASS THEMSELVES.

WE WERE POOR, WITH DIGNITY.

JORGE'S CHILDHOOD APPEARS TO HAVE
BEEN A HAPPY ONE. HIS ITALIAN-ARGENTINE
GRANDMOTHER ROSA DOTED ON HIM AND
HIS SIBLINGS. HE PLAYED SOCCER
PASSIONATELY BUT NOT VERY WELL.

FRIENDS REMEMBER THAT HE WAS MORE AT
HOME WITH HIS HEAD BURIED IN A BOOK.

FROM HIS SCHOOLS TO HIS STREETS, FROM HIS FAMILY TO HIS FRIENDS, JORGE EXPERIENCED A FUNDAMENTAL AND PRIVILEGED SERENITY THAT HAS POWERFULLY SHAPED HIS DEMEANOR AND PERSPECTIVE. I FIRST FELT IT AT THE PARK IN FLORES, BUT I EXPERIENCED IT AGAIN AND AGAIN AS I MOVED THROUGH HIS WORLD.

Mark K. Shriver, author of Pilgramage: My Search for the Real Pope Francis

ARGENTINA'S MOVE TO THE POLITICAL LEFT
WAS A BIG INFLUENCE ON JORGE DURING HIS
FORMATIVE YEARS.

PROMISING SOCIAL JUSTICE AND ECONOMIC
INDEPENDENCE FROM COLONIALISM, THE
CHARISMATIC JUAN PERÓN BECAME
PRESIDENT FOLLOWING A POPULAR UPRISING
IN 1946, WHEN JORGE WAS NINE. IN THE
ENSUING YEARS, PERÓN NATIONALIZED
BANKS AND PUBLIC WORKS AND EXPANDED
THE SOCIAL SAFETY NET. WAGES ROSE.

IT'S HARD TO KNOW WHAT JORGE THOUGHT OF PERÓN'S POLITICS AT THE TIME. BUT HE WAS DEVOUT AND THE GOVERNMENT WAS CLOSELY ALIGNED WITH THE CHURCH, AT LEAST UNTIL THE MID-1950s.

LIKE MOST ARGENTINES, JORGE PROBABLY LOOKED FAVORABLY ON THE REGIME'S POLICIES, WHICH INCLUDED BIG INCREASES IN SOCIAL SPENDING.

AT AGE TWELVE OR THIRTEEN JORGE BEGAN
THINKING OF BECOMING A PRIEST "IN THE
WAY THAT YOU THINK ABOUT BEING AN
ENGINEER, A DOCTOR, OR A MUSICIAN."

BUT THE FUTURE POPE FRANCIS SAYS HE
FELT HIS FIRST STRONG CALLING TO THE
CHURCH AT AGE SIXTEEN. IT WAS SEPTEMBER
21, 1953 -- THE FIRST DAY OF SPRING IN THE
SOUTHERN HEMISPHERE -- AND HE DECIDED
TO DROP BY HIS PARISH CHURCH FOR
CONFESSION.

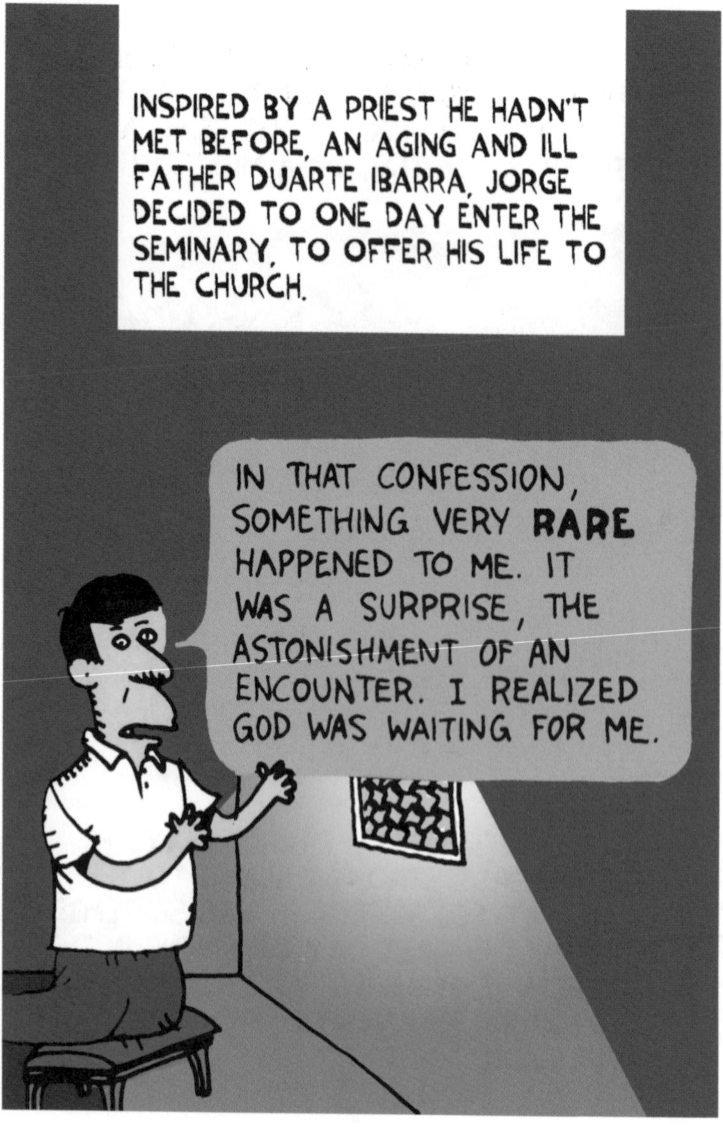
INSPIRED BY A PRIEST HE HADN'T MET BEFORE, AN AGING AND ILL FATHER DUARTE IBARRA, JORGE DECIDED TO ONE DAY ENTER THE SEMINARY, TO OFFER HIS LIFE TO THE CHURCH.
IN THAT CONFESSION, SOMETHING VERY RARE HAPPENED TO ME. IT WAS A SURPRISE, THE ASTONISHMENT OF AN ENCOUNTER. I REALIZED GOD WAS WAITING FOR ME.

PERÓN Y EVITA

A SUS QUERIDOS DESCAMISADOS LES DESEAN
FELIZ NAVIDAD Y AÑO NUEVO
1949-1950

ONE FRIEND REMEMBERS JORGE GETTING IN
TROUBLE FOR WEARING A PRO-PERÓN
BADGE TO SCHOOL. ANOTHER INSISTS
JORGE WAS ALWAYS ANTI-PERÓN, HOWEVER.

JORGE HELD VARIOUS JOBS TO PAY HIS
BILLS AND HELP HIS FAMILY. HE SWEPT
FLOORS AS A JANITOR AND DID CLERICAL
WORK AT A HOSIERY FACTORY WHERE HIS
FATHER WAS AN ACCOUNTANT. PRESAGING
HIS INTEREST IN SCIENCE -- A KEY ASPECT
OF THE JESUIT ORDER -- JORGE SERVED AS
A TECHNICIAN IN THE FOODS SECTION AT
HICKETHIER-BACHMANN LABORATORY. HE
EVENTUALLY GRADUATED FROM TECHNICAL
SCHOOL AS A CHEMICAL TECHNICIAN.

ONE OF THE GREAT
VIRTUES OF THE SCIENCES
IS HUMILITY. BEING A
SCIENTIST MEANS THAT
YOU HAVE TO EMBRACE
THE FACT THAT YOU
DON'T KNOW EVERYTHING.

Alex Knapp, Forbes

PEOPLE ARE AMUSED TO LEARN THAT THE
FUTURE POPE FRANCIS WAS ALSO A
BOUNCER AT A BAR.

JORGE WAS GREGARIOUS AND ENERGETIC.
LIKE MOST YOUNG ARGENTINE MEN OF THE
TIME, HE WENT OUT DANCING, CHASED GIRLS
(THOUGH LACKADAISICALLY), AND
FOLLOWED SOCCER. BUT HE KNEW IT
WOULDN'T LAST. AT THE CHEMICAL PLANT
HIS FRIEND OSCAR CRESPO, WHO ALSO
WORKED THERE, RECALLS THAT JORGE TOLD
HIM:

"I'M GOING TO FINISH
SECONDARY SCHOOL
WITH YOU GUYS, BUT
I'M NOT GOING TO BE
A CHEMIST, I'M GOING
TO BE A **PRIEST**. BUT
I'M NOT GOING TO BE A
PRIEST IN A BASILICA.
I'M GOING TO BE A
JESUIT, BECAUSE I'M
GOING TO WANT TO GO
OUT TO THE NEIGHBOR-
HOODS, TO THE VILLAS,
TO BE WITH PEOPLE."

AT AGE EIGHTEEN HE ENTERED THE
ARCHDIOCESAN SEMINARY, INMACULADA
CONCEPCIÓN SEMINARY, IN VILLA DEVOTO
IN BUENOS AIRES. AT THE SAME TIME, AN
INCREASINGLY PARANOID, REPRESSIVE, AND
AUTHORITARIAN PERÓN SPLIT FROM THE
CHURCH. A MILITARY COUP FORCED PERÓN
INTO EXILE, SETTING THE STAGE FOR
DECADES OF REPRESSION, DURING WHICH
PERÓN'S PARTY WAS BANNED.

FROM THE 1950s TO THE 1970s
ARGENTINA WAS PARALYZED BY A
POLITICAL PARADOX THAT IS HARD
FOR FOREIGNERS TO GRASP: THE
ANTILIBERALS (THE NATIONALISTS,
PERÓNISTS) WERE POPULAR AND CAME
TO POWER BY WINNING ELECTIONS,
WHILE THE LIBERALS — THE DEMOCRATS,
THE PLURALISTS — USED DICTATORSHIP
TO KEEP THE PERÓNISTS OUT OF POWER.

Austen Ivereigh, Francis's biographer

THREE YEARS LATER, ON MARCH 11, 1958,
JORGE ENTERED THE SOCIETY OF JESUS
(THE JESUITS) IN SANTIAGO, CHILE, WHERE HE
STUDIED HUMANITIES AS A NOVICE. HE WAS
TWENTY-ONE.

HIS NICKNAME AT SEMINARY: EL GRINGO
(POSSIBLY BECAUSE OF HIS ITALIAN
HERITAGE).

BERGOGLIO WITH HIS MOTHER

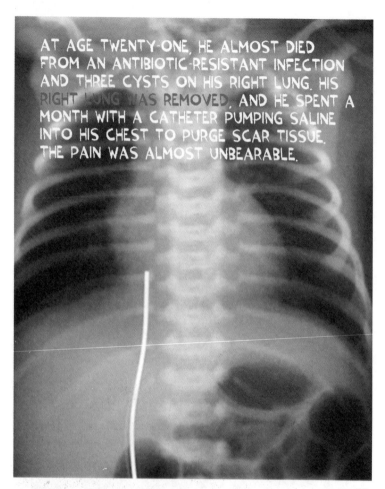

AT AGE TWENTY-ONE, HE ALMOST DIED FROM AN ANTIBIOTIC-RESISTANT INFECTION AND THREE CYSTS ON HIS RIGHT LUNG. HIS RIGHT LUNG WAS REMOVED, AND HE SPENT A MONTH WITH A CATHETER PUMPING SALINE INTO HIS CHEST TO PURGE SCAR TISSUE. THE PAIN WAS ALMOST UNBEARABLE.

MEDICINE

Why Pope Francis Only Has One Lung

Pope Francis is a pioneering pontiff in many ways — he's the first to take the name of Francis, the first pope from South America, and the first to don the papal robes with an unusual medical condition.

BERGOGLIO HAD HIS DOUBTS ABOUT A LIFE OF CELIBACY. WHILE AT SEMINARY HE FELL SO HARD FOR A BEAUTIFUL, INTELLIGENT GIRL HE MET AT HIS UNCLE'S WEDDING THAT HE CONSIDERED DROPPING HIS RELIGIOUS CAREER.

[PEOPLE] WANT THEIR CAKE AND TO EAT IT TOO.

BECOMING A CATHOLIC PRIEST REQUIRES
ROUGHLY A DECADE OF STUDY. IN 1960
(AGE TWENTY-THREE), BERGOGLIO FINISHED
HIS TWO YEARS AS A JESUIT NOVITIATE
AND TOOK THE REQUIRED VOWS OF
POVERTY, CHASTITY, AND OBEDIENCE.
THERE WAS NO TURNING BACK.

THAT SAME YEAR, HE EARNED HIS LICENTIATE
(THE ARGENTINE EQUIVALENT OF A MASTER'S
DEGREE) IN PHILOSOPHY AT COLEGIO MÁXIMO
DE SAN JOSÉ, A JESUIT RELIGIOUS COLLEGE IN
SAN MIGUEL, ARGENTINA. AS THE ARGENTINE
POLITICAL SCENE CAME TO A BOIL AS A
RESULT OF THE ONGOING CLASH BETWEEN THE
ARMY AND THE PERÓNISTS, MANY OF
BERGOGLIO'S PEERS LEFT THE JESUIT ORDER
TO DO ACTIVE LEFT-WING POLITICAL WORK.
BERGOGLIO FELT MORE MOTIVATED THAN
EVER.

AT AGE TWENTY-SEVEN, HE TOOK A JOB AS
A TEACHER AT A JESUIT HIGH SCHOOL. FROM
1964 TO 1965 THE FUTURE POPE TAUGHT
SPANISH AND ARGENTINE LITERATURE AND
PSYCHOLOGY AT THE COLEGIO DE LA
INMACULADA CONCEPCIÓN IN SANTA FE,
ARGENTINA. STUDENTS REMEMBER HIM AS
LIKEABLE AND GIFTED WITH A SHARP
INTELLECT.

HE MOVED TO THE COLEGIO DEL SALVADOR
IN BUENOS AIRES IN 1966.

NICKNAME: CARUCHA (LONG FACE) BECAUSE
OF HIS MOURNFUL EXPRESSION.

IN 1967 BERGOGLIO COMPLETED HIS THEOLOGICAL STUDIES AT THE SEMINARY FACULTADES DE FILOSOFÍA Y TEOLOGÍA DE SAN MIGUEL (PHILOSOPHICAL AND THEOLOGICAL FACULTY OF SAN MIGUEL). THERE, TOO, HE WAS POPULAR AND ENGAGING.

THE GREAT THING ABOUT BERGOGLIO WAS THAT **NO DOORS WERE CLOSED.**

-- Jorge Milia
Former student

"[Marxism is] alien not only to Christianity but to the spirit of our [Argentine] people."

—Declaration of San Miguel, issued by Argentina's bishops in 1969

todos con
PERON—PERON
SINDICATO DEL SEGURO
de la REPUBLICA ARGENTINA

AS BERGOGLIO WAS ORDAINED TO THE PRIESTHOOD ON DECEMBER 13, 1969, AND WENT TO WORK AT SAN MIGUEL AS A THEOLOGY PROFESSOR, HE WAS ENTERING A BRANCH OF THE CHURCH THAT, CONFRONTED WITH A CHOICE BETWEEN MARXISM-INFLUENCED LIBERATION THEOLOGY AND AUTHORITARIANISM, WAS ALLYING ITSELF WITH THE FORCES OF REACTION, EVEN AS IT EMPHASIZED PEOPLE AS ACTIVE AGENTS OF THEIR OWN HISTORY.

CHURCH OFFICIALS NOTICED THE BRIGHT AND CHARISMATIC YOUNG JESUIT PRIEST. HE ROSE QUICKLY THROUGH THE JESUIT BUREAUCRACY, AIDED IN NO SMALL PART BY A HIGHER-THAN-USUAL NUMBER OF YOUNG JESUITS LEAVING THE ORDER TO JOIN THE LEFT-WING POLITICAL STRUGGLE. ONE VACANCY OPENED UP AFTER ANOTHER. THE OLD GUARD WAS DETERMINED TO GIVE JORGE'S NEW GENERATION A CHANCE TO LEAD.

BY 1973, HE WAS PUT IN CHARGE OF THE JESUIT COMMUNITY OF ARGENTINA AS A "PROVINCIAL SUPERIOR." HE WASN'T READY.

HE SAID HE WAS TOO YOUNG, TOO INEXPERIENCED, TOO AUTHORITARIAN, PEOPLE SAID HE WAS AN ULTRA-CONSERVATIVE BECAUSE OF THE WAY HE BEHAVED. HE REGRETTED THAT.

Paul Vallely
author of Pope
Francis: The Struggle
for the Soul of
Catholicism

THAT WAS **CRAZY**. I HAD TO DEAL WITH DIFFICULT SITUATIONS, AND I MADE MY DECISIONS ABRUPTLY AND BY MYSELF.

IT WAS A DARK TIME FOR ARGENTINA. A RIGHT-WING MILITARY JUNTA SEIZED POWER IN 1976 AND ESTABLISHED AUTHORITARIAN RULE. CONGRESS WAS CLOSED, THE PRESS WAS CENSORED, AND UNIONS WERE BANNED.

IT WAS ALSO HARD FOR CATHOLICS. THE MILITARY REGIME WAS DETERMINED TO CONTROL THE CHURCH. IT WAS IMPOSSIBLE TO OPERATE INDEPENDENTLY. SOME RESISTED, BUT ENDED UP DYING UNDER SUSPICIOUS CIRCUMSTANCES, SUCH AS CONVENIENTLY TIMED CAR CRASHES.

THE ARGENTINE CHURCH WAS ONE OF THE MOST CONSERVATIVE IN LATIN AMERICA. IT SHOWED A GOOD DISPOSITION TOWARD THE MILITARY AUTHORITIES...

Sergio Rubín
Pope Francis's authorized biographer

DIRTY WAR

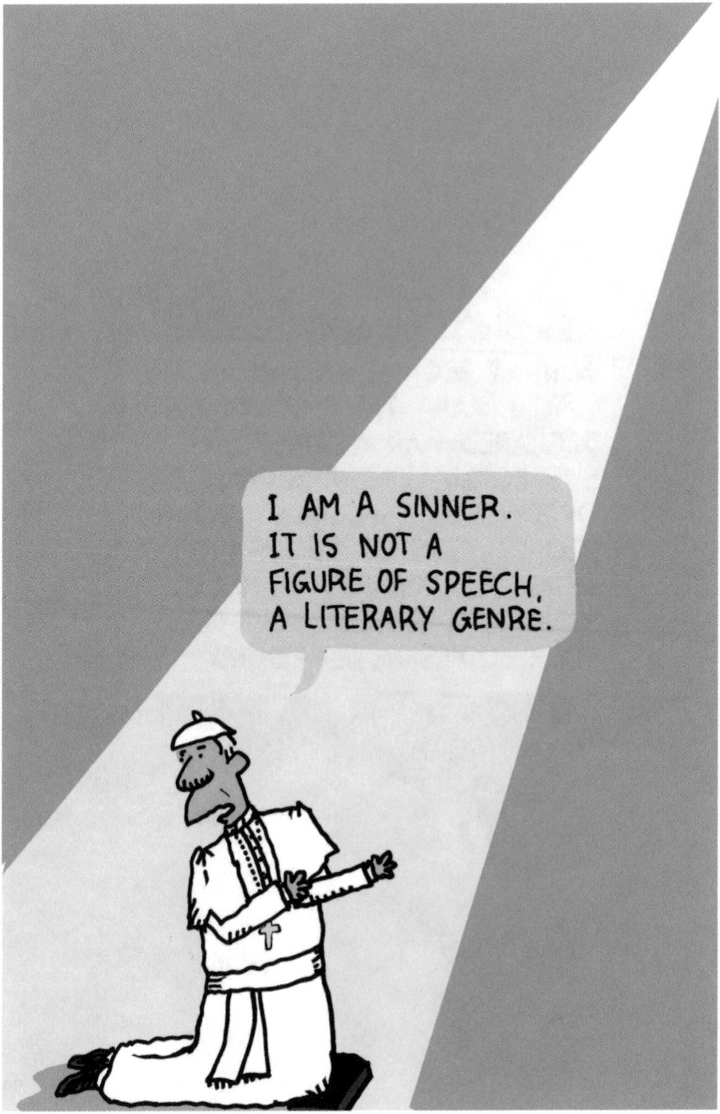
I AM A SINNER. IT IS NOT A FIGURE OF SPEECH, A LITERARY GENRE.

IN WHAT BECAME KNOWN AS THE "DIRTY WAR," THE DICTATORSHIP DECLARED WAR AGAINST SUSPECTED LEFT-WING POLITICAL OPPONENTS, ESPECIALLY YOUNG PEOPLE. TENS OF THOUSANDS WERE "DISAPPEARED" -- KILLED WITHOUT A TRACE, MOST OF THEIR BODIES NEVER FOUND.

THE OPPOSITION LEFT
RADICALIZED INTO FACTIONS,
INCLUDING ARMED GUERRILLA
GROUPS. DETERMINED TO RESIST,
REVOLUTIONARY LEFTISTS
BOMBED RIGHT-WING "CLASS
ENEMIES."

ARGENTINE PRIESTS WERE DRAWN TO ONE OF THE TWO STRAINS OF LIBERATION THEOLOGY. BOTH GAVE PREFERENCE TO THE POOR: ONE CALLED FOR REFORM, WHILE THE OTHER FOUGHT TO OVERTHROW THE GOVERNMENT IN A COMMUNIST REVOLUTION.

ARGENTINA'S CATHOLIC HIERARCHY WAS DEEPLY CONSERVATIVE. MANY, INCLUDING BERGOGLIO, HAD TIES TO THE GOVERNMENT, ITS ARMED PARAMILITARY ALLIES, AND POSSIBLY EVEN THOSE IN CHARGE OF TORTURE CENTERS.

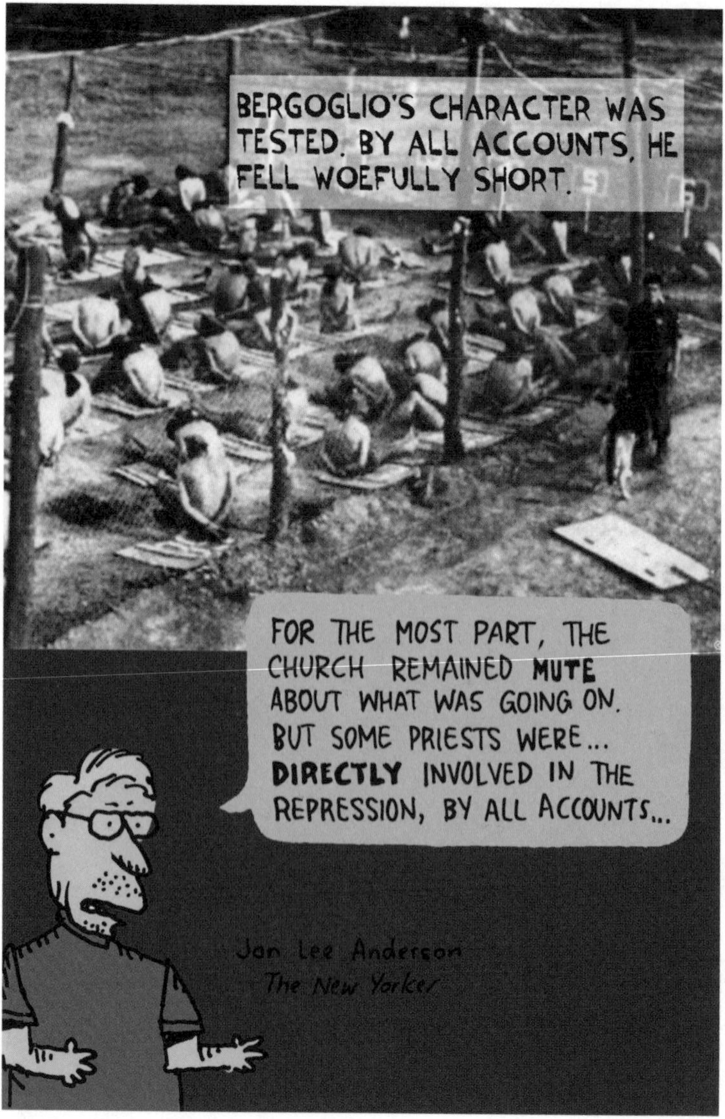
BERGOGLIO'S CHARACTER WAS TESTED. BY ALL ACCOUNTS, HE FELL WOEFULLY SHORT.
FOR THE MOST PART, THE CHURCH REMAINED **MUTE** ABOUT WHAT WAS GOING ON. BUT SOME PRIESTS WERE... **DIRECTLY** INVOLVED IN THE REPRESSION, BY ALL ACCOUNTS...
Jon Lee Anderson
The New Yorker

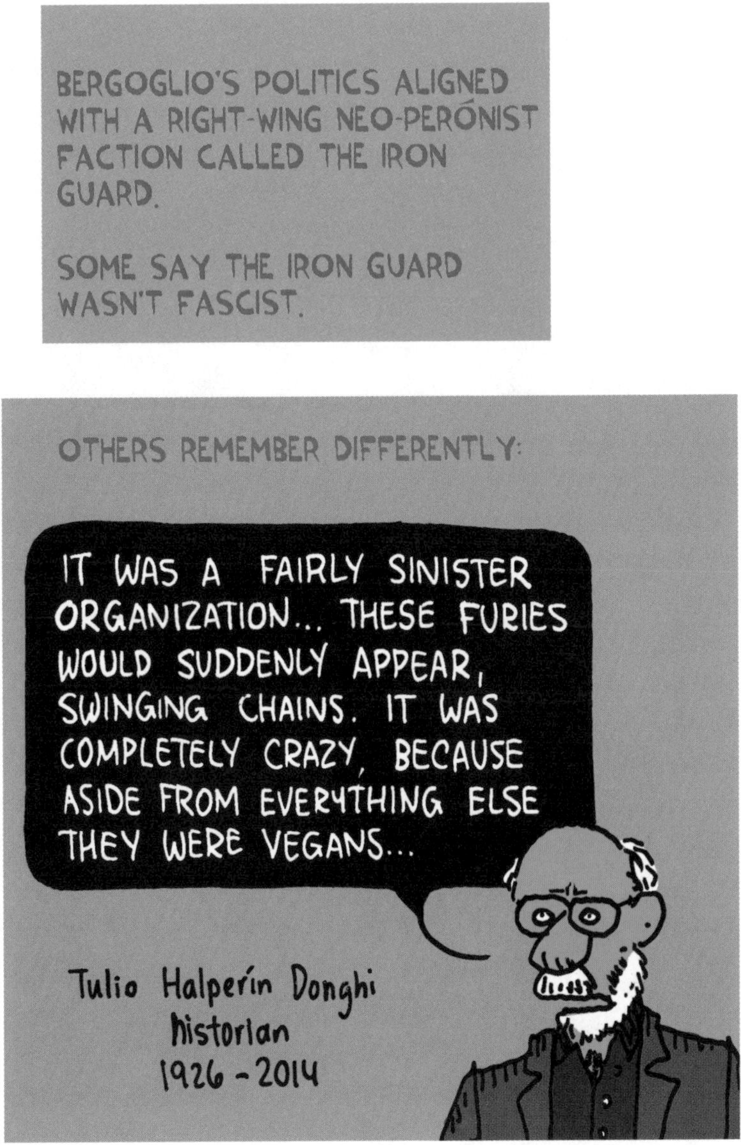
BERGOGLIO'S POLITICS ALIGNED WITH A RIGHT-WING NEO-PERÓNIST FACTION CALLED THE IRON GUARD.
SOME SAY THE IRON GUARD WASN'T FASCIST.
OTHERS REMEMBER DIFFERENTLY:
IT WAS A FAIRLY SINISTER ORGANIZATION... THESE FURIES WOULD SUDDENLY APPEAR, SWINGING CHAINS. IT WAS COMPLETELY CRAZY, BECAUSE ASIDE FROM EVERYTHING ELSE THEY WERE VEGANS...
Tulio Halperín Donghi
historian
1926 - 2014

TRYING TO STREAMLINE THE JESUIT ORDER'S FINANCES AND OPERATIONS LED BERGOGLIO TO A DECISION FOR WHICH MANY ON THE LEFT NEVER FORGAVE HIM.

SINCE THERE WERE TWO JESUIT UNIVERSITIES IN BUENOS AIRES, HE DECIDED TO TURN OVER ONE OF THEM (WHICH WAS IN DEBT) TO A SECULAR ENTITY: A GROUP OF MEN WHO HAD BELONGED TO THE IRON GUARD BEFORE ITS SUBSEQUENT DISSOLUTION.

TWO JESUITS IN BERGOGLIO'S ORDER,
HUNGARIAN-BORN FRANZ JALICS AND THE
ARGENTINE ORLANDO YORIO, SUFFERED AS
THE RESULT OF BERGOGLIO'S TENURE. THE
TWO ACTIVIST PRIESTS WERE HIS FORMER
PHILOSOPHY AND THEOLOGY PROFESSORS.

THEY WERE ORGANIZING THE POOR IN THE
VILLAS MISERIA OF BUENOS AIRES. THEY SAID
THEY WERE APOLITICAL.

AT THE REQUEST OF THE MILITARY, BERGOGLIO
TOLD THEM TO STOP. THEY DISOBEYED HIS
ORDER, SO HE EXPELLED THEM FROM THE
JESUITS. THE ARCHBISHOP OF BUENOS AIRES
AUTOMATICALLY WITHDREW THEIR RIGHT TO
SAY MASS.

THEY SPENT FIVE MONTHS BLINDFOLDED, IN CHAINS, NEARLY STARVED IN FILTHY CELLS.

THE MILITARY LOOKED AT THIS AND SAID "THESE MEN HAVE BEEN TOSSED ASIDE BY THEIR OWN ORDER AND BY THE HIERARCHY OF THE CHURCH..." THEY TORTURED THEM... THERE WAS A LOT OF ILL FEELING IN THE JESUITS THAT [BERGOGLIO] LET THESE MEN DOWN.

Paul Vallely

POPE FRANCIS MAINTAINS THAT THE ARRESTS WEREN'T HIS FAULT.

I WARNED THEM TO BE VERY CAREFUL. THEY WERE TOO EXPOSED TO THE PARANOIA OF THE WITCH HUNT. BECAUSE THEY STAYED IN THE BARRIO, YORIO AND JALICS WERE KIDNAPPED.

YORIO, NOW DEAD, REMAINED BITTER FOR YEARS, SAYING HIS *PROVINCIAL* BERGOGLIO BETRAYED HIM AND THREW HIM TO THE WOLVES.

I HAVE NO REASON TO BELIEVE HE DID ANYTHING TO FREE US, IN FACT JUST THE OPPOSITE.

JALICS REFUSES TO COMMENT, SAYING THE
MATTER WAS SETTLED. HOWEVER, POPE
FRANCIS MET WITH HIM YEARS LATER AND
THEY CELEBRATED MASS TOGETHER IN A
GESTURE OF FORGIVENESS.

MOREOVER, FORMER MEMBERS OF THE IRON
GUARD VOUCH FOR BERGOGLIO, SAYING HE
PULLED STRINGS WITH DICTATOR JORGE
RAFAEL VIDELA TO SPARE THE TWO PRIESTS'
LIVES. INDEED, ALL THE OTHER JESUITS
ARRESTED THAT WEEK WERE "DISAPPEARED."

SO WHAT DID BERGOGLIO DO DURING THE DIRTY WAR? THE QUESTION CARRIES ECHOES OF SIMILAR CONCERNS ABOUT THE CHURCH'S POSITION DURING WORLD WAR II.

AFTER 1945, PEOPLE IN COUNTRIES LIKE FRANCE -- GOVERNED BY THE NAZI-COLLABORATIONIST VICHY REGIME -- HAD TO EXPLAIN WHY THEY DIDN'T RESIST OR, IF THEY DID, WHY NO ONE CAN VERIFY THAT THEY FOUGHT BACK WHEN IT REALLY MATTERED.

BERGOGLIO'S LEGACY IS MURKY. THOUGH HE PLAYED FOOTSIE WITH THE IRON GUARD, HE ALSO HELPED SEVERAL GUERRILLA FIGHTERS, SOME FROM NEIGHBORING URUGUAY, HIDE OR FLEE THE COUNTRY. HE EVEN CLAIMS TO HAVE GIVEN HIS NATIONAL ID PAPERS TO A MAN WHO LOOKED LIKE HIM SO HE COULD ESCAPE TO BRAZIL.

PERHAPS HE DIDN'T HAVE THE COURAGE OF OTHER PRIESTS, BUT HE NEVER COLLABORATED WITH THE DICTATORSHIP. BERGOGLIO WAS NO ACCOMPLICE OF THE DICTATORSHIP.

Adolfo Pérez Esquivel, who won the 1980 Nobel Peace Prize for documenting the junta's atrocities

THERE'S HYPOCRISY HERE WHEN IT COMES TO THE CHURCH'S CONDUCT, AND WITH BERGOGLIO IN PARTICULAR.

THERE ARE TRIALS OF ALL KINDS NOW, AND BERGOGLIO... REFUSES TO SUPPORT THEM.

Estela de la Cuadra, whose mother cofounded the Grandmothers of the Plaza de Mayo activist group to search for missing family members

DE LA CUADRA SAYS HER FAMILY, WHICH LOST FIVE RELATIVES TO GOVERNMENT THUGS, APPROACHED THE LEADER OF THE JESUITS IN ROME TO TRY TO SAVE ESTELA'S SISTER ELENA. SHE WAS FIVE MONTHS PREGNANT WHEN SHE WAS KIDNAPPED IN 1977.

ROME URGED BERGOGLIO TO HELP. BERGOGLIO ASSIGNED A MONSIGNOR TO MEET WITH THE POLICE. BECAUSE ELENA WAS A COMMUNIST, THEY SAID, SHE WOULD BE EXECUTED. IN PRISON, HOWEVER, SHE HAD GIVEN BIRTH TO A GIRL. THE BABY WAS HANDED OVER TO A FAMILY FOR ADOPTION. IN 2010 BERGOGLIO DENIED KNOWING ANYTHING ABOUT STOLEN BABIES.

BERGOGLIO HAS A VERY COWARDLY ATTITUDE... THE PEOPLE KNOW HOW HE IS.

IN 1980, BERGOGLIO RETURNED TO THE PHILOSOPHICAL AND THEOLOGICAL FACULTY OF SAN MIGUEL AS RECTOR FOLLOWING HIS SEVEN-YEAR SPELL AS PROVINCIAL SUPERIOR OF ARGENTINA'S JESUITS. THE DIRTY WAR WAS WINDING DOWN.

THE WORST ATROCITIES HAD PASSED AND, SHORTLY AFTER THE ARGENTINE JUNTA'S DEFEAT BY THE BRITISH IN THE FALKLANDS WAR, DEMOCRACY WOULD BE RESTORED. BUT HE LEFT THE ARGENTINE JESUIT COMMUNITY DEEPLY DIVIDED INTO PRO- AND ANTI-BERGOGLIO FACTIONS.

IN 1986 ROME DISPATCHED JESUIT SUPERIOR-GENERAL PETER HANS KOLVENBACH OF THE NETHERLANDS TO HEAL THE RIFT. AS BERGOGLIO'S TERM AS RECTOR ENDED, HE WAS SENT AWAY TO GERMANY, THEN RETURNED TO ARGENTINA TO TEACHING DUTIES. AFTER BERGOGLIO BEGAN TO VOICE DISAPPROVAL WITH THE WAY HIS PEERS WERE RUNNING THE SCHOOL WHERE HE TAUGHT, HE WAS REASSIGNED TO A SCHOOL DISTANT FROM BUENOS AIRES, IN CORDOBA. KOLVENBACH WAS DISPLEASED WITH BERGOGLIO'S DOGMATIC CONSERVATISM.

THOSE EVENTS DON'T APPEAR IN CHURCH NARRATIVES. ACCORDING TO HIS BIOGRAPHER AUSTEN IVEREIGH, KOLVENBACH FORMALLY ACCUSED BERGOGLIO OF DIRECTING JESUIT STUDENTS TO REACH OUT TO INDIVIDUAL PARISHES AND BY ENGAGING IN POPULAR RELIGIOSITY. OFFICIAL JESUIT POLICY AT THE TIME WAS TO PROMOTE SOCIAL JUSTICE VIA SCIENTIFIC SOCIOLOGICAL ANALYSIS.

BERGOGLIO'S PRE-PAPAL CAREER ALLOWED
HIM TO TRAVEL EXTENSIVELY. HE WENT TO
ISRAEL IN 1973, BUT THE OUTBREAK OF THE
YOM KIPPUR WAR FORCED HIM TO REMAIN
CONFINED TO HIS HOTEL FOR THE MAJORITY
OF THE TRIP.

HE SPENT THREE MONTHS IN DUBLIN IN 1980
ON SABBATICAL, ATTENDING THEOLOGY
CLASSES WHILE LEARNING THE ENGLISH
LANGUAGE.

AFTER BEING DISMISSED AS RECTOR OF SAN
MIGUEL, HE WENT TO FRANKFURT, GERMANY,
TO RESEARCH POSSIBLE DISSERTATION
TOPICS. HE BECAME MORE WORLDLY, MORE
OPEN TO OTHER POINTS OF VIEW.

NEVERTHELESS, FRANCIS'S UNDERSTANDING OF WHAT IT MEANT TO BE A MEMBER OF THE SOCIETY OF JESUS REMAINED CONSERVATIVE TO THE POINT OF BEING ORIGINALIST.

AS RECTOR OF SAN MIGUEL HE ENFORCED A "SANDALS YES, BOOKS NO" BACK-TO-THE-PEOPLE APPROACH.

BERGOGLIO PRIVILEGED POPULAR RELIGIOSITY AND THE WORK OF THE YOUNG PEOPLE IN POPULAR PARISHES WHILE NEGLECTING THE RESEARCH CENTERS... IT WAS...MORE PERÓNIST THAN MODERN.

Father Fernando Montes

GOD WORKED IN ME THROUGH THOSE MISTAKES.

PERHAPS THE GREATEST IRONY OF BERGOGLIO'S LIFE IS THAT A MAN WHO TORE APART HIS NATIVE COUNTRY'S JESUIT ORDER BECAUSE HE WAS PERCEIVED AS BEING A CONSERVATIVE ALLY OF A NOTORIOUS JUNTA EVOLVED INTO WHAT MOST CATHOLICS CONSIDER TO BE THE MOST RADICAL-LEFT PONTIFF OF THEIR LIFETIMES.

FRANCIS IS FAMOUS AS THE FIRST JESUIT POPE. IN YET ANOTHER IRONY, DESPITE HIS CLAIMS TO HAVE DISOBEYED THE JUNTA BY SUPPORTING POPULAR RELIGIOSITY DURING THE DIRTY WAR, BERGOGLIO FELT HE WAS PUNISHED BY THE ORDER FOR BEING REACTIONARY. FROM 1990 TO 1992, HE WAS VIRTUALLY EXILED TO CÓRDOBA ON ACCOUNT OF HIS STATUS AS A "DISSENTER" AND HIS OPPOSITION TO LIBERATION THEOLOGY. HIS PRESENCE IN BUENOS AIRES, BERGOGLIO'S SUPERIORS SEEM TO HAVE BELIEVED, WAS DISRUPTIVE.

BERGOGLIO'S BRAND OF POPULAR RELIGIOSITY WAS OUT. OVER TIME, THE LIBERATION THEOLOGY FACTION REGAINED CONTROL.

LITTLE BY LITTLE THE APOSTOLATE WAS ABANDONED, AND IN JUST A FEW YEARS THE CHURCHES WERE REDUCED TO THE BARE MINIMUM, AMONG OTHER THINGS BECAUSE THERE WAS A POLICY OF "CLEANSING" THE *BERGOGLIANO* JESUITS.

Austen Ivereigh

FRANCIS'S INTELLECTUAL LIFE REMAINS DEEPLY INFLUENCED BY JESUIT ATTITUDES AND RELIANCE ON LOGIC AND REASON WITHIN THE FRAMEWORK OF FAITH. HOWEVER, FOR SEVERAL YEARS, HE HAD LITTLE CONTACT WITH THE CLERGY HE ONCE KNEW. THIS WAS A RESULT OF HIS ACTIONS (AND INACTIONS) DURING THE DIRTY WAR, AND HIS TOUGH MANAGEMENT STYLE.

WHEN I SPOKE WITH FELLOW JESUITS FROM OTHER COUNTRIES ABOUT BERGOGLIO'S PROSPECTS FOR BECOMING POPE, I WAS TAKEN ABACK BY THEIR DISLIKE... THE ALIENATION BETWEEN BERGOGLIO AND THE JESUITS WAS A THORN IN HIS SIDE THAT HE BORE WITH SILENT PATIENCE.

Margaret Hebblethwaite
The Guardian

Call the exorcist: pope tells priests to consult experts in casting out demons

Pope Francis advised confessors to refer to an exorcist to better address parishioners' who have 'real spiritual disorders' with supernatural origins

FRANCIS BELIEVES IN SCIENCE. YET HE ADHERES TO TRADITIONAL VIEWS OF RELIGION THAT MANY BELIEVE SHOULD BEST BE FORGOTTEN AS VESTIGES OF MEDIEVAL CHURCH HISTORY. IN 2017 HE ADVISED PRIESTS NOT TO HESITATE TO CALL ON VATICAN-TRAINED EXORCISTS IF ONE OF THEIR FLOCK FELL VICTIM TO DEMONIC POSSESSION.

PENANCE

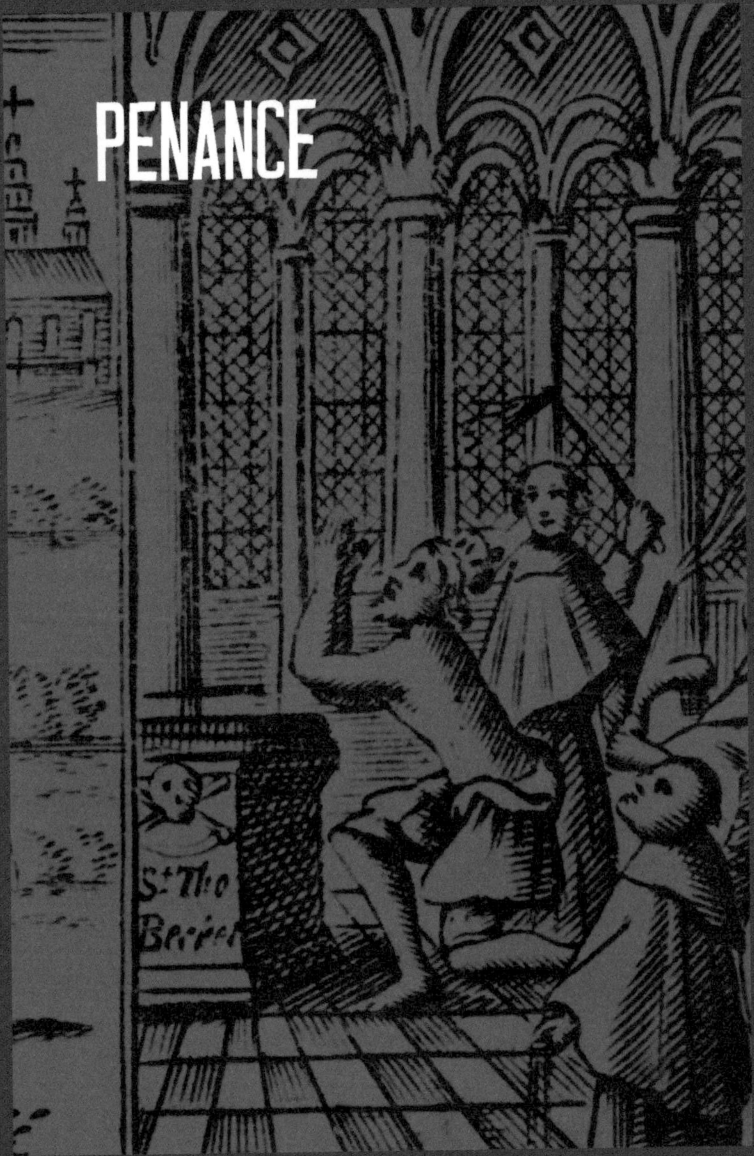
St Tho

BERGOGLIO'S ESTRANGEMENT FROM HIS FELLOW JESUIT *PORTEÑOS* WAS PAINFUL. BUT IT WAS ACTUALLY GOOD FOR HIS CAREER, BRINGING HIM CLOSER TO THE MAINLINE CHURCH HIERARCHY IN ROME.

CARDINAL ANTONIO QUARRACINO OF BUENOS AIRES APPOINTED HIM ASSISTANT BISHOP OF BUENOS AIRES IN 1992, THEN IN 1998 HE SUCCEEDED QUARRACINO AS BUENOS AIRES'S ARCHBISHOP.

BERGOGLIO WAS SIXTY-TWO YEARS OLD.

MAYBE A BAD JESUIT CAN BECOME A GOOD BISHOP.

an anonymous Jesuit

THE FACT THAT HE HAD BEEN SOMEWHAT REJECTED, INTERNALLY, BY THE JESUITS, IF NOT FOR THAT HE PROBABLY WOULD NOT HAVE BECOME A BISHOP.

Father Humberto Miguel Yanez
Argentine Jesuit head of the moral
theology dept. at Gregorian U. in Rome

THE STONE THAT THE BUILDERS REJECTED BECAME THE CORNERSTONE.

Paraphrasing
Matthew 21: 42-44

192

AS BISHOP, BERGOGLIO MOURNED HIS ESTRANGEMENT FROM THE ARGENTINE JESUITS EVEN AS HE SOUGHT TO LEARN FROM THE EXPERIENCE.

"...THE FIRST ANSWER THAT COMES TO ME IS USUALLY WRONG. I DON'T HAVE ALL THE ANSWERS. I DON'T EVEN HAVE ALL THE QUESTIONS. I ALWAYS THINK OF NEW QUESTIONS, AND THERE ARE ALWAYS NEW QUESTIONS COMING FORWARD."

THE DIRTY WAR WAS OVER FOR ARGENTINA. BUT BERGOGLIO FELT HE OWED PENANCE. THAT BELIEF WOULD INFORM THE REST OF HIS LIFE.

IT WAS HARD NOT TO THINK OF THE DISPUTE HE'D HAD WITH THE TWO "SLUM PRIESTS" WHO WERE TORTURED DURING THE DIRTY WAR WHEN ONE OF HIS MAJOR INITIATIVES AS ARCHBISHOP WAS TO EXPAND THE CHURCH'S PRESENCE IN POOR NEIGHBORHOODS. HE MORE THAN DOUBLED THE NUMBER OF PRIESTS STATIONED IN THE SLUMS.

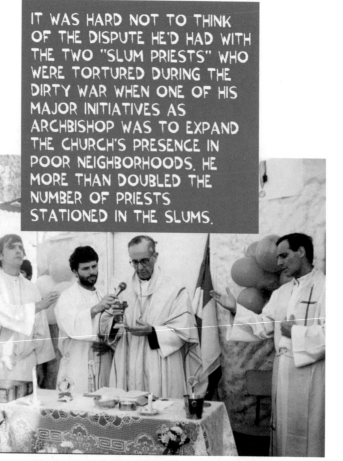

THAT, AND HIS FREQUENT VISITS TO SHANTYTOWNS, EARNED HIM THE NICKNAME "THE SLUM BISHOP."

IN 2000 ARCHBISHOP BERGOGLIO SAID THE ENTIRE ARGENTINE CHURCH SHOULD CLAD ITSELF IN GARMENTS OF PUBLIC PENANCE FOR THE SINS OF THE DIRTY WAR.

THAT DIDN'T HAPPEN, OF COURSE. BUT HIS STATEMENT HIGHLIGHTS HIS BELIEF THAT ARGENTINA SHOULD NOT SWEEP THE DIRTY WAR UNDER THE RUG.

Argentine Tells of Dumping 'Dirty War' Captives Into Sea

Pilots charged with Argentina dirty war 'death flights'

INSIDE ARGENTINA'S SECRET DEATH CAMPS

IN 2001 POPE JOHN PAUL II APPOINTED HIM
CARDINAL-PRIEST OF SAN ROBERTO
BELLARMINO, A CHURCH IN ROME RUN BY
JESUITS. LATER THAT YEAR, HE WAS
APPOINTED GENERAL RELATOR (RECORDING
SECRETARY) IN THE SYNOD OF BISHOPS.
THERE, ACCORDING TO THE *CATHOLIC
HERALD*, HE CREATED "A FAVOURABLE
IMPRESSION AS A MAN OPEN TO
COMMUNION AND DIALOGUE."

LATER THE SAME YEAR, CARDINAL
BERGOGLIO AUTHORIZED A
REQUEST FOR BEATIFICATION --
THE FIRST STEP TOWARD
SAINTHOOD -- FOR THE THREE
PRIESTS AND TWO SEMINARIANS
MURDERED DURING THE DIRTY WAR
BY THE ARGENTINE JUNTA IN THE
SAN PATRICIO CHURCH MASSACRE.

HE ORDERED AN INVESTIGATION
INTO THE MURDERS AS WELL.

Argentina

Pope Francis orders Vatican to open files on Argentina dictatorship

● Papal nuncio had close relationship with 1976-83 military junta
● Argentinian pontiff acts after meeting with one of mothers of 'disappeared'

IN ROME THE NEW CARDINAL
EARNED A REPUTATION FOR
HUMILITY, DOCTRINAL
CONSERVATISM, AND AN ARDENT
BELIEF IN THE FIGHT FOR SOCIAL
JUSTICE.

PASSING UP THE LUXURIOUS
RESIDENCE TO WHICH HE WAS
ENTITLED, HE LIVED IN A SMALL
APARTMENT, TOOK PUBLIC
TRANSPORTATION, DRESSED IN
USED GARMENTS, AND COOKED HIS
OWN MEALS.

SERIOUSLY. REALLY. DON'T CONSIDER ME FOR THIS. SOMEONE ELSE WOULD BE BETTER. ANYONE ELSE WOULD BE BETTER.

IN THE VOTE FOR THE NEXT POPE FOLLOWING JOHN PAUL II'S DEMISE, BERGOGLIO NEVER TRAILED VERY FAR BEHIND RATZINGER.

WANTING TO AVOID A PROTRACTED SUCCESSION BATTLE, HE MADE A PASSIONATE, NEARLY TEARFUL PLEA TO HIS FELLOW CARDINALS, URGING THEM NOT TO VOTE FOR HIM.

IN HIS CAPACITY AS CHAIRMAN OF THE
ARGENTINE CATHOLIC BISHOPS' CONFERENCE,
BERGOGLIO APOLOGIZED FOR THE CHURCH'S
ROLE IN THE DIRTY WAR.

HE TURNED SEVENTY-FIVE IN DECEMBER
2011, THE AGE AT WHICH CANON LAW
DICTATES BISHOPS MUST SUBMIT THEIR
RESIGNATION, AND HE DUTIFULLY
FULFILLED HIS OBLIGATION.

BUT BECAUSE HE HAD NO COADJUTOR
BISHOP, HE REMAINED IN OFFICE WHILE
AWAITING A REPLACEMENT APPOINTED BY
THE VATICAN.

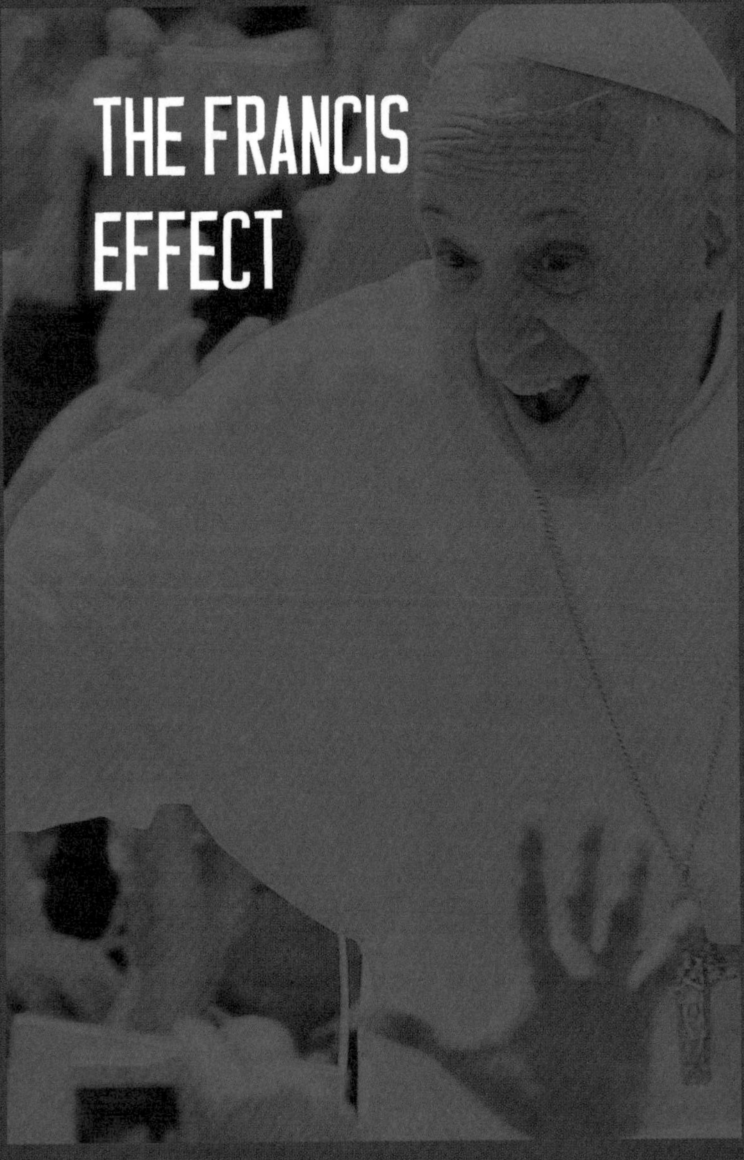
THE FRANCIS
EFFECT

LEFT-LEANING CATHOLICS HAVE BEEN LARGELY SATISFIED WITH FRANCIS'S PAPACY, ESPECIALLY WITH HIS CRITICISM OF GROWING INCOME INEQUALITY AND ECONOMIC INJUSTICE.

"The grave financial and economic crises of the present time . . . have pushed man to seek satisfaction, happiness and security in consumption and earnings out of all proportion to the principles of a sound economy. The succession of economic crises should lead to a timely rethinking of our models of economic development and to a change in lifestyles."

—Pope Francis, 2013

Pope more popular than world leaders

HE IS AN EXCEEDINGLY POPULAR POPE.

"Eighty-five percent of Catholics and 60 percent of non-Catholics view the pope favorably, numbers that would make politicians green with envy."

—*National Catholic Reporter* March 6, 2014

Pope Francis' popularity among Americans goes from high to higher

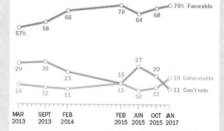

Seven-in-ten U.S. adults view Pope Francis favorably

% of U.S. adults who say their opinion of Pope Francis is ...

POPULAR POPE: FRANCIS GETS BETTER POLL RATINGS THAN OBAMA AND MERKEL

204

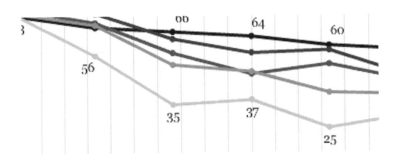

HE HAS EXCITED CATHOLICS AT A TIME WHEN THE PHRASE "LAPSED CATHOLIC" HAS ALMOST BECOME STANDARD.

CHURCH ATTENDANCE, CONSISTENTLY DECLINING SINCE THE 1950s, HAS REMAINED STEADY SINCE FRANCIS BECAME POPE.

Trends in Self-Reported Mass Attendance Among U.S. Catholics

	Weekly or more	Less often	Don't know
	%	%	%
2007	41	58	1=100
2008	43	57	1=100
2009	41	59	1=100
2010	40	59	1=100
2011	38	62	1=100
2012	40	59	1=100
2013	39	60	1=100

PEWS AREN'T FILLING UP. BUT THEY'RE NOT GETTING EMPTIER EITHER. AND THAT'S AN ACCOMPLISHMENT.

"Although most Catholics report no change, 26 percent of Catholics are more excited about their faith; 40 percent are praying more; and 21 percent are reading the Bible more."

—*National Catholic Reporter*
March 6, 2014

Catholic World News

Pope confirms: Amoris Laetitia allows divorced/remarried to receive Communion in some cases

BUT NOT EVERYTHING IS SWEETNESS AND LIGHT IN THE AGE OF POPE FRANCIS. IN 2016, FRANCIS ISSUED HIS APOSTOLIC STATEMENT ON LOVE AND ROMANTIC RELATIONSHIPS IN WHICH HE SAID BISHOPS COULD ALLOW CATHOLICS WHO HAVE DIVORCED AND REMARRIED IN A CIVIL CEREMONY TO TAKE COMMUNION -- A MAJOR DEPARTURE FROM PREVIOUS POLICY.

MANY LAY CATHOLICS WERE PLEASED.

IN AN ECHO OF MARTIN LUTHER, DISSENT CAME IN THE PERSON OF A CONSERVATIVE FROM GERMANY -- FRANCIS'S OWN CHIEF OF DOCTRINE, GERHARD LUDWIG MÜLLER.

SOME CATHOLIC WATCHERS SAY THE CONDITIONS ARE RIPE FOR A CRISIS -- PERHAPS EVEN ANOTHER SCHISM.

NO POWER IN HEAVEN OR ON EARTH, NEITHER AN ANGEL, **NOR THE POPE,** NOR A COUNCIL, NOR A LAW OF THE BISHOPS, HAS THE FACULTY TO CHANGE IT.

Conservative opposition to Pope Francis spurs talk of a schism in the Catholic Church

Could a pope be in schism?

The plot against the Pope

It is no secret in Rome that several cardinals want Francis to step down

HONDURAN CARDINAL ÓSCAR MARADIAGA NOTED THAT AMONG THE CONSERVATIVE HIERARCHY COULD BE HEARD EXPRESSIONS LIKE "WHAT CAN IT BE THAT THIS LITTLE ARGENTINE PRETENDS?"

". . . there are high-ranking and increasingly outspoken discontents both within the Curia and abroad—a number of U.S. bishops among them—who are deeply unhappy with what they believe is the pope's betrayal of the Catholic faith; so unhappy, in fact, that, according to my friend [in the Vatican], some are even contemplating the possibility of establishing a separate Catholicism. The man who would unite all religions in a shared belief in God's love, and who as *provincial* of the Argentine Jesuits so divided his order that outside intervention was required, is again proving his ability to unite and divide."
—Alma Guillermoprieto, *Matter*

FOR THE TIME BEING, COOLER HEADS SEEM LIKELY TO PREVAIL.

HIS OPPONENTS LOST POWER WITH RATZINGER'S RESIGNATION...THE POPE CAN DO WHAT HE LIKES.

Giacomo Galeazzi
Vatican Insider

FRANCIS IS A REFORMER, NOT A REVOLUTIONARY.

HE'S NOT URGING CHANGES IN DOCTRINE, ONLY SUBTLE CALLS FOR FLEXIBILITY IN INTERPRETATION, LIKE AN "ASK ME NO QUESTIONS AND I'LL TELL YOU NO LIES" POLICY FOR CATHOLICS WHO HAVE COMMITTED WHAT THE CHURCH CONSIDERS SINS -- LIKE GETTING DIVORCED, OR USING BIRTH CONTROL.

PETITIONER: ANG

RESPONDENT: WILLIAM B

Petitioner requests that the court make the following or

5. LEGAL GROUNDS (Family Code sections 2200–2210.

a. ☑ Divorce or ☐ Legal separation of th
   (1) ☑ irreconcilable differences. (2) ☐

b. ☐ Nullity of void marriage or domestic partnersh
   (1) ☐ incest. (2) ☐ bigamy.

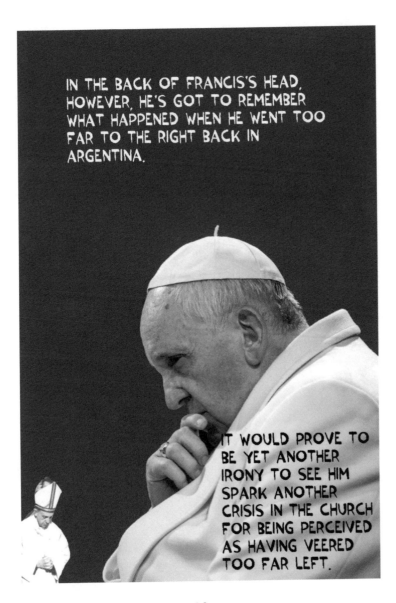

IN THE BACK OF FRANCIS'S HEAD, HOWEVER, HE'S GOT TO REMEMBER WHAT HAPPENED WHEN HE WENT TOO FAR TO THE RIGHT BACK IN ARGENTINA.

IT WOULD PROVE TO BE YET ANOTHER IRONY TO SEE HIM SPARK ANOTHER CRISIS IN THE CHURCH FOR BEING PERCEIVED AS HAVING VEERED TOO FAR LEFT.

IN THE MEANTIME, FRANCIS LABORS ON WITH GESTURES LIKE PRESSING HIS PALM AGAINST ISRAEL'S "SECURITY WALL" ALONG ITS BORDER WITH THE PALESTINIAN TERRITORIES. JUST LIKE THAT, HE SEEMED TO DRAW AN EQUIVALANCE TO THE WAILING WALL IN JERUSALEM, SACRED TO JEWS.

The pope's visit confounded many, and maybe that was the point

Francis, Peres, Abbas: A pope, two presidents and a prayer for peace

Pope Francis gets warm welcome from Palestinians

Vatican to Recognize Palestinian State in New Treaty

Francis calls for end to 'unacceptable' Israeli-Palestinian conflict

IT WASN'T A BOLD DECLARATION THAT PALESTINE DESERVED STATEHOOD. BUT, BECAUSE HE IS POPE, IT PUT PRESSURE ON ISRAEL TO CONSIDER RESUMING LONG-STALLED PEACE TALKS.

FRANCIS LEVERAGES HIS MORAL AUTHORITY TO EFFECT POLITICAL CHANGE.

AFTER HALF A CENTURY OF SUBJECTING POST-REVOLUTIONARY CUBA TO INVASIONS, COVERT SABOTAGE, AND ECONOMIC EMBARGO, THE US AGREED TO LIFT TRAVEL RESTRICTIONS AND MOVE TOWARD NORMALIZED RELATIONS IN 2014.

Pope Francis bridged gap between U.S. and Cuba during secret talks

Pope Francis credited for urging U.S., Cuba to normalize relations

How Pope Francis' diplomacy may change everything, not just US–Cuba relations

MONTHS LATER, NEWS LEAKED THAT PRESIDENT OBAMA HAD AGREED TO REOPEN TALKS WITH CUBA WHEN POPE FRANCIS REQUESTED THAT HE DO SO THE FIRST TIME THEY MET.

IN 2017 POPE FRANCIS EVEN WENT AFTER THE MAFIA. SORRY, TONY SOPRANO! AT THE VATICAN'S FIRST "INTERNATIONAL DEBATE ON CORRUPTION," CHURCH OFFICIALS SAID MOBSTERS WOULD HAVE TO CHOOSE BETWEEN ORGANIZED CRIME AND ORGANIZED RELIGION.

News › World › Europe

Pope Francis I excommunicates Mafia for 'adoration of evil' in strongest attacks in 20 years

Visiting southern Italy after one of infamous group's most shocking killings, Pope Francis said that the church would use all of its power to combat organised crime

Pope Francis

Pope Francis to mafia: repent or 'end up in hell'

Pope Francis made the

Francis's stance on organised crime in contrast with church's perceived former reluctance to criticise mafia bosses

FRANCIS HAS SINCE FOCUSED ON CONSOLIDATING HIS PAPACY.

WITHIN THE COUNCIL OF CARDINALS HE IS PUSHING FOR SUCH MAJOR STRUCTURAL REFORMS AS THE ORDINATION OF MARRIED PRIESTS, LONG PERMITTED BY PROTESTANTS.

WE MUST THINK... [WHETHER] *VIRI PROBATI* ARE A POSSIBILITY.

older married men who are already involved in church brsiness

HE ORDERED A COMMISSION TO INVESTIGATE ALLOWING WOMEN DEACONS.

THIS WILL COME AS A SURPRISE EVEN TO
LAY CATHOLICS, BUT THIS "PRO-LIFE"
CHURCH'S MOST RECENT CATECHISM (1992)
STILL PERMITS THE DEATH PENALTY UNDER
SOME CIRCUMSTANCES. POPE FRANCIS
CALLED FOR A CHANGE THAT EVOKED THE
DEBATE BETWEEN AMERICA'S
CONSTITUTIONAL ORIGINALISTS AND THOSE
WHO BELIEVE THE DOCUMENT IS ALIVE AND
SUBJECT TO RENEWED INTERPRETATION.

"The Word of God cannot be conserved in
mothballs as if it were an old blanket to be
preserved from parasites. No. The Word
of God is a dynamic reality, always alive,
that progresses and grows because it
tends towards a fulfillment that men
cannot stop."
--Pope Francis

"It is necessary therefore to restate that,
however grave the crime that may have been
committed, the death penalty is inadmissible
because it attacks the inviolability and the
dignity of the person."

HE CONTINUED TO INSERT HIMSELF INTO
INTERNATIONAL POLITICS MORE
AGGRESSIVELY THAN HIS PREDECESSORS.
WITH A NUCLEAR STANDOFF BETWEEN THE
U.S. AND NORTH KOREA ESCALATING INTO A
WAR OF INSULTS BETWEEN THE TWO
COUNTRIES' LEADERS, FRANCIS CONVENED A
CONFERENCE CALLING FOR AN END TO THE
COLD WAR-ERA APPROACH TO NUCLEAR
WEAPONS OF DETERRENCE. THE GOAL, THE
POPE SAID, SHOULD BE TOTAL NUCLEAR
DISARMAMENT.

Trump trades 'short and fat' barb with N Korea's Kim

© 12 November 2017 US & Canada   f y ● ☑ < Share

Pope Francis wants to save the world from nuclear crisis

Kim Jong-un and Donald Trump

On nuclear weapons, Pope Francis goes beyond all previous papal teaching

WEAPON OF HOLY MASS
DESTRUCTION **Pope Francis wades into North Korea crisis and vows to save the world from nuclear disaster**

Holyman to give a talk to gathering of UN and Nato officials as well as Nobel Peace Prize winners as tensions with North Korea continue

THOUGH IN GOOD HEALTH, FRANCIS IS AWARE OF HIS AGE: HE IS ENTERING HIS EIGHTIES. DETERMINED THAT HIS REFORMS OUTLAST HIM, HE PURGED THE VATICAN OF CONSERVATIVES, REPLACING THEM WITH PROGRESSIVE-MINDED LEADERS.

IN JULY 2017 HE OUSTED CARDINAL GERHARD LUDWIG MÜLLER, THE TOP DOCTRINAL WATCHDOG WHOSE RESISTANCE TO FRANCIS HAD PROMPTED SOME OBSERVERS TO WORRY ABOUT A SCHISM. ARCHBISHOP LUIS LADARIA, SEVENTY-THREE, A SPANISH JESUIT THEOLOGIAN, TOOK HIS PLACE.

Rev. James Martin, editor-at-large, America magazine, and a consulter to the Vatican's Secretariat for Communication

THIS GIVES THE POPE THE CHANCE TO FINALLY PLACE HIS OWN MAN IN A VERY IMPORTANT SPOT...CARDINAL MÜLLER WAS THE LAST LINK TO BENEDICT'S WAY OF DOING THINGS.

MANY PEOPLE CONSIDER POPE BENEDICT XVI'S RETIREMENT SHAMEFUL. NOT FRANCIS. HE SAYS HE WOULD CONSIDER DOING THE SAME.

"Our span of life increases and at a certain age we no longer have the ability to govern well because our body is weary; our health may be good but we don't have the ability to deal with all the problems of a government like that of the Church. I believe that Pope Benedict XVI took this step which de facto instituted popes emeriti . . . You can ask me: 'What if one day you don't feel prepared to go on?' I would do the same, I would do the same! I will pray hard over it, but I would do the same thing. [Benedict] opened a door which is institutional, not exceptional."

BUT THERE'S NO SIGN OF THAT YET. FRANCIS
REMAINS ACTIVE. HE TRAVELS ABROAD
FREQUENTLY. AND IT WOULD BE STRANGE
FOR THERE TO BE TWO POPES EMERITI.

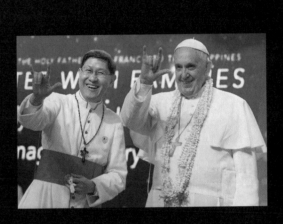

ODDS ARE, FRANCIS WILL CONTINUE TO
REFORM CHURCH DOCTRINE AND REPLACE
PERSONNEL. HE IS INTERESTED IN GROOMING
A SUCCESSOR WHO WOULD CONTINUE TO
MODERNIZE THE CHURCH. FOR EXAMPLE, LUIS
ANTONIO TAGLE, ARCHBISHOP OF MANILA, IS
ONLY FIFTY-EIGHT -- AND HE'S AN ACOLYTE
OF FRANCIS. HE IS PRESIDENT OF CARITAS,
THE CATHOLIC RELIEF NETWORK. THIS GIVES
TAGLE INTERNATIONAL EXPOSURE AND
COULD HELP HIM AT THE NEXT CONCLAVE.

OF COURSE, FRANCIS WILL DRAW ON HIS
HONESTY TO MAKE STATEMENTS SURPRISING
FOR THEIR WIT AND DOWN-TO-EARTH
HUMANISM, AS WHEN HE SAID THAT YOU
SHOULDN'T ASK A PANHANDLER HOW HE
PLANS TO USE THE MONEY WHEN YOU GIVE
HIM ALMS.

"THERE ARE MANY EXCUSES [NOT TO GIVE
MONEY TO A BEGGAR. SOME MAY THINK] 'I
GIVE MONEY AND HE JUST SPENDS IT ON A
GLASS OF WINE!' [IF] A GLASS OF WINE IS
THE ONLY HAPPINESS HE HAS IN LIFE, THAT'S
O.K. INSTEAD, ASK YOURSELF, WHAT DO
YOU DO ON THE SLY? WHAT 'HAPPINESS'
DO YOU SEEK IN SECRET? [GIVING TO
SOMEONE IN NEED] IS ALWAYS RIGHT."

SOMETIMES, TO MAKE HIS POINT, ALL HE HAS TO DO IS SHOW UP.

HIS MEETING WITH NEWLY ELECTED PRESIDENT DONALD TRUMP DIDN'T ACCOMPLISH MUCH POLITICALLY. BUT IT WAS WIDELY REMARKED UPON FOR THE JUXTAPOSITION BETWEEN THESE TWO MEN.

ONE HUMBLE, ONE GAUDY. ONE WORRIED ABOUT CLIMATE CHANGE, THE OTHER A GLOBAL WARMING DENIALIST. ONE WHO URGES THAT REFUGEES BE WELCOMED, THE OTHER WHO WANTS TO BUILD A WALL AND ORDERS MASS DEPORTATIONS.

POPE FRANCIS CALLS OUT TRUMP, ACCUSES HIM OF "PRO-LIFE" HYPOCRISY

Pope Francis Criticized the U.S. for Pulling out of the Paris Climate Accord

Pope Francis criticizes Trump's stance on DACA

TRUMP LOOKED SMALLER THAN EVER.

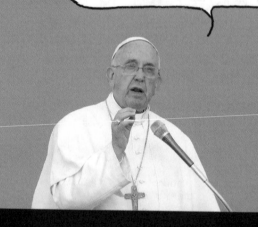

IF I SAY I AM CATHOLIC AND GO TO MASS, BUT THEN DON'T SPEAK TO MY PARENTS, HELP MY GRAND-PARENTS OR THE POOR, GO AND SEE THOSE WHO ARE SICK, THIS DOES NOT PROVE MY FAITH, THERE'S NO POINT. THOSE WHO DO THIS ARE NOTHING BUT CHRISTIAN PARROTS - WORDS, WORDS, WORDS.

ULTIMATELY, FRANCIS IS THE CEO OF GLOBAL CATHOLICISM. MORE THAN HIS RECENT PREDECESSORS, HE SEEKS TO REMIND US OF WHAT CHRISTIANITY WAS ORIGINALLY ABOUT.

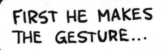

Father Antonio Spadaro, Jesuit interviewer of Pope Francis

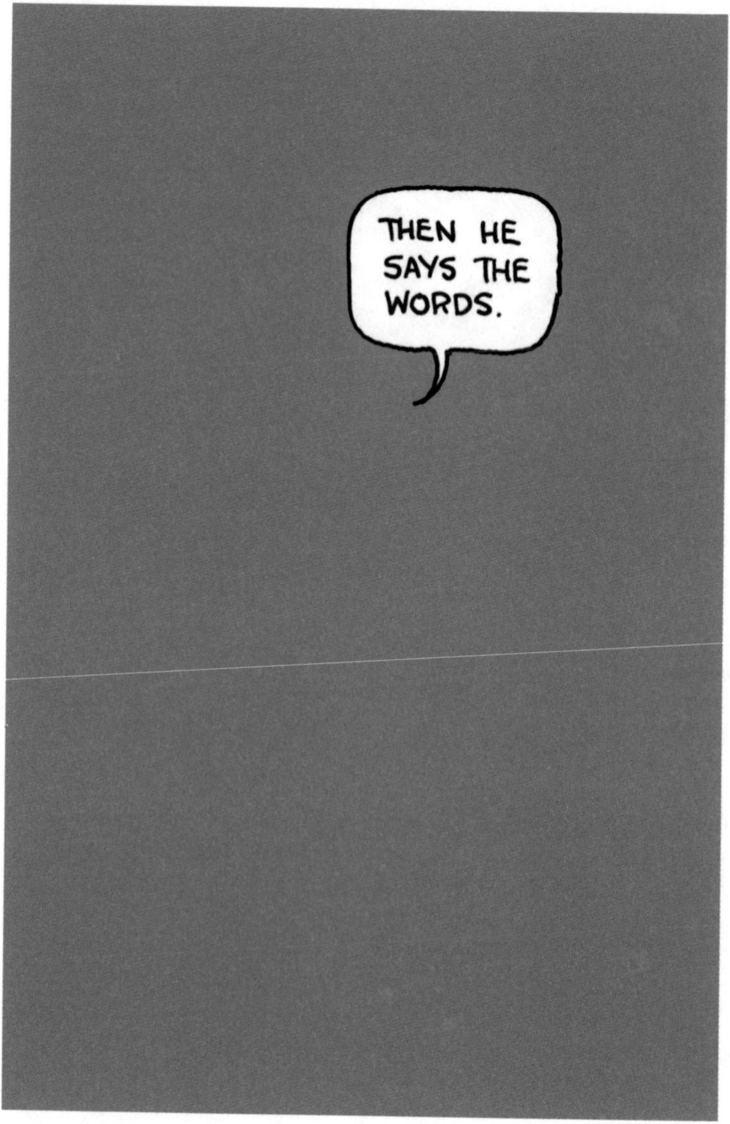
THEN HE SAYS THE WORDS.

Afterword

The world was shocked, but mostly pleasantly surprised, by the election of a relatively unknown cardinal named Jorge Mario Bergoglio as pope in 2013. But it probably won't shock you, dear reader, to learn that it didn't happen by chance.

A powerful movement within the papal conclave to replace the abdicated Pope Benedict XVI originated with a Vatican version of the United States Senate's "Gang of Eight"—an informal group of powerful reform-minded cardinals who pulled strings and leaned on contacts within the conclave and the Curia in order to get Bergoglio the throne of Saint Peter.

The so-called St. Gallen mafia was accused, falsely it seems, of plotting to depose Benedict. But they did play an important role in pushing Bergoglio. "They first secured Bergoglio's assent," wrote Francis biographer Austen Ivereigh. "Asked if he was willing, he said that he believed that at this time of crisis for the Church no cardinal could refuse if asked. Murphy-O'Connor knowingly warned him to 'be careful,' and that it was his turn now, and was told 'capisco'—'I understand.'

"Then they got to work, touring the cardinals' dinners to promote their man, arguing that his age—seventy-six—should no longer be considered an obstacle, given that popes could resign."

Cardinal Theodore McCarrick, archbishop emeritus of Washington, DC, said six months after Francis's election that the plotters gave Pope Francis five years to reform the Roman Catholic Church. McCarrick quoted a man he described as highly positioned—so probably part of the St. Gallen mafia: "[Bergoglio] could reform the Church. If we gave him five years, he could put us back on target."

McCarrick says he replied: "But he's seventy-six."

The man said: "Yeah, five years. If we had five years, the Lord working through Bergoglio in five years could make the Church over again."

It has been five years. Has Pope Francis Made the Church Great Again?

He has his detractors. But he has certainly tried to carry out significant reforms.

As Thomas J. Reese wrote in the *National Catholic Reporter*, "This pope communicates in a way that grabs people's attention with his words and actions . . . He does not obsess over rules and regulations. He is more interested in orthopraxis (how we live the faith) than orthodoxy (how we explain the faith)."

Like Pope John XXIII, Francis is interested in open debate over practices, interpretations of scripture, and even dogma. This seemed impossible under John Paul II and Benedict XVI.

He has placed concern for the environment front and center at a time when global governments, especially in the United States, seem unable to act.

From the standpoint of the St. Gallen mafia, who wanted to see major reforms, Francis has been a success. From the Vatican Bank to the Curia to urging church officials to see themselves as servants of God and of the people rather than as autocrats, Francis has promoted transparency.

There remains, of course, the question of Francis's age. If seventy-six was a concern, eighty-one is more so. Francis seems healthy and energetic and certainly sharp-minded, but he is now officially in demographic overtime. Every day is a gift. At some point, inevitably, as we all will, Francis will pass and another group of red-suited cardinals will gather for a conclave in the sacred halls of the Vatican to choose his replacement. As we saw with the retrograde papacies of John Paul II and Benedict XVI, it is easy for progress to be rolled back, for ossification and corruption to take root anew. It's a parallel to the vision of the Bible, which describes one final epic battle between good and evil only in the anomalous Book of Revelation. Mostly, Christianity centers around an ongoing war between the two, final victory never being in the cards for either because that would deny humanity its free will. Francis has changed a great deal. The question is, will his reforms, and his Church, last in our rapidly changing world?

TED RALL

Notes

7. Cindy Wooden, "Pope Francis Explains Why He Chose St. Francis of Assisi's Name," Catholic News Service, March 17, 2013, http://www.catholicnews.com/services/englishnews/2013/pope-francis-explains-why-he-chose-st-francis-of-assisi-s-name.cfm.

8. Avery Dulles, "What Distinguishes the Jesuits?," America: The Jesuit Review, Vol. 196 No. 2 (January 15, 2007), http://www.americamagazine.org/issue/599/article/what-distinguishes-jesuits.

9. Stephanie Watson, Pope Francis: First Pope from the Americas (Minneapolis, MN: Lerner Publications Company, 2014).

10. Max Fisher, "Sorry, Jose Mario Bergoglio is Not the First Non-European Pope," Washington Post, March 13, 2013, https://www.washingtonpost.com/news/worldviews/wp/2013/03/13/sorry-jorge-mario-bergoglio-is-not-the-first-non-european-pope.

12. Dennis Coday, "Pope's Quotes: No Small Chapel," National Catholic Reporter, October 14, 2013, https://www.ncronline.org/blogs/francis-chronicles/pope-s-quotes-no-small-chapel.

12. Nick Squires, "Pope Francis Shunned Official Papal Apartments to Live 'Normal Life,'" Telegraph, May 29, 2013, http://www.telegraph.co.uk/news/worldnews/the-pope/10086876/Pope-Francis-shunned-official-papal-apartments-to-live-normal-life.html.

12. Agence France Presse, "Pope Francis Eschews Tradition with Silver Ring," Capital News, March 18, 2013, http://www.capitalfm.co.ke/news/2013/03/pope-francis-eschews-tradition-with-silver-ring/.

13. CNA/EWTN News, "Many Accuse Pope Francis of Socialist, Even Communist Leanings—Is He?," Catholic Online, July 23, 2015, http://www.catholic.org/news/hf/faith/story.php?id=62261.

13. Zachary A. Goldfarb and Michelle Boorstein, "Pope Francis Denounces 'Trickle-Down' Economic Theories in Sharp Criticism of Inequality," *Washington Post*, November 26, 2013, https://www.washingtonpost.com/business/economy/pope-francis-denounces-trickle-down-economic-theories-in-critique-of-inequality/2013/11/26/e17ffe4e-56b6-11e3-8304-caf30787c0a9_story.html?utm_term=.6b8cca386286.

14. Hari Sreenivasan and John Allen, "Pope Francis Reforms Scandal-Ridden Vatican Bank in Hopes of Making It 'Boringly Successful,'" *PBS NewsHour*, July 9, 2014, http://www.pbs.org/newshour/bb/pope-francis-reforms-scandal-ridden-vatican-bank-hopes-making-boringly-successful.

14. Daniel Burke and Kristi Ramsay, "Pope Francis on Sexual Abuse: 'God Weeps,'" CNN, September 27, 2015, http://www.cnn.com/2015/09/27/us/pope-francis-sex-abuse-victims/index.html.

14. Rod Dreher, "Priest: Here's Why Bishops Cover Up Abuse," American Conservative, February 4, 2013, http://www.theamericanconservative.com/dreher/priest-bishops-cover-up.

14. Joe Mahr and Mitch Weiss, "Authorities Abetted Diocese in Hiding Sexual-Abuse Cases," *Toledo Blade*, July 31, 2005, http://www.toledoblade.com/frontpage/2005/07/31/Authorities-abetted-diocese-in-hiding-sexual-abuse-cases.html.

14. Daniel Burke and Kristi Ramsay, "Pope Francis on Sexual Abuse: 'God Weeps,'" CNN, September 27, 2015, http://www.cnn.com/2015/09/27/us/pope-francis-sex-abuse-victims/index.html.

15. Quoted in John L. Allen Jr., "Pope on Homosexuals: 'Who Am I to Judge?'" *National Catholic Reporter*, July 29, 2013, https://www.ncronline.org/blogs/ncr-today/pope-homosexuals-who-am-i-judge.

16. Michael O'Loughlin, "Pew Survey: Percentage of US Catholics Drops and Catholicism is Losing Members Faster Than Any Denomination," Crux, May 12, 2015, https://cruxnow.com/church/2015/05/12/pew-survey-percentage-of-us-catholics-drops-and-catholicism-is-losing-members-faster-than-any-denomination/.

17. Bill Press, *Buyer's Remorse: How Obama Let Progressives Down* (New York: Simon & Schuster, 2016).

22. Amelia Monroe Carlson, "5 Reasons the Catholic Church is the True Church," Catholic365.com, June 24, 2015, http://www.catholic365.com/article/1723/5-reasons-the-catholic-church-is-the-true-church.html.

22. "Was Peter in Rome?" Catholic Answers, August 10, 2004, https://www.catholic.com/tract/was-peter-in-rome.

23. A. Van Hove, "Bishop," *The Catholic Encyclopedia: An International Work of Reference on the Constitution, Doctrine, Discipline, and History of the Catholic Church, Vol. II*, eds. Charles G. Herbermann, et al. (New York: The Universal Knowledge Foundation, 1913), 581–89 [581].

23. Jonathan Wynne-Jones, "St. Peter Was Not the First Pope and Never Went to Rome, Claims Channel 4," *Telegraph*, March 23, 2008, http://www.telegraph.co.uk/news/worldnews/1582585/St-Peter-was-not-the-first-Pope-and-never-went-to-Rome-claims-Channel-4.html.

23. Jaroslav Jan Pelikan, Martin E. Marty, and Michael Frassetto, "Roman Catholicism: The Age of Reformation and Counter-Reformation," *Encyclopædia Britannica*, July 26, 1999, last updated October 27, 2016, https://www.britannica.com/topic/Roman-Catholicism/The-age-of-Reformation-and-Counter-Reformation.

23. "Global Christianity—A Report on the Size and Distribution of the World's Christian Population," Pew Research Center, December 19, 2011, http://www.pewforum.org/2011/12/19/global-christianity-exec/.

24. Christopher Klein, "10 Things You May Not Know About the Vatican," History.com, March 12, 2013, http://www.history.com/news/10-things-you-may-not-know-about-the-vatican.

24. Muhammad Wajid Akhter, "The End: The Anniversary of the Abolition of the Caliphate," MuslimMatters, June 24, 2010, http://muslimmatters.org/2010/06/24/the-end-the-anniversary-of-the-abolition-of-the-caliphate/.

25. The Treaty of Tordesillas of 1494, negotiated by Pope Alexander VI, divided South America between Spanish and Portuguese areas of control. "Treaty of Tordesillas," *Encyclopædia Britannica*, July 20, 1998, last updated November 4, 2014, https://www.britannica.com/event/Treaty-of-Tordesillas.

25. In 800 AD, for example, Pope Leo III crowned Charlemagne the Holy Roman Emperor, making him the most powerful man in the world. Matthias von Hellfeld, "Charlemagne is Crowned Emperor—December 25, 800," DW (Deutsche Welle), November 16, 2009, http://www.dw.com/en/charlemagne-is-crowned-emperor-december-25-800/a-4614858-1.

Perhaps the most famous example of papal delegitimation occurred in 1077, when Holy Roman Emperor Henry IV trekked across the Alps to beg forgiveness from Pope Gregory VII. Gregory, who had excommunicated

Henry (and decreed that his subjects were no longer required to obey him) for usurping his authority by appointing his own bishops, made Henry wait three days in the snow before letting him into his castle and forgiving him. Three years later, however, the piqued Henry deposed Gregory, forcing him into exile. Claire Suddath, "Top 10 Apologies: Mea Culpa—Emperor Henry IV," *Time*, September 7, 2010, http://content.time.com/time/specials/packages/article/0,28804,1913028_1913030_1913049,00.html.

25. During the Thirty Years' War (1618–1648), for example, a German civil conflict drew in European alliances based on religious affiliations, pitting Catholics against Protestants. At least three million people died. Elliot [Mashhadi], "10 Bloodiest Wars in History," Eskify, undated, http://eskify.com/10-bloodiest-wars-in-history.

26. "State Departments," Vatican City State, undated, http://www.vaticanstate.va/content/vaticanstate/en/stato-e-governo/organi-dello-stato.html.

27. "Catechism of the Catholic Church: Part Two—The Celebration of the Christian Mystery, Section Two—The Seven Sacraments of the Church, Chapter Two—The Sacraments of Healing," Holy See, undated, http://www.vatican.va/archive/ccc_css/archive/catechism/p2s2c2a4.htm.

27. Deacon Keith Fournier, narrator, "Prayer during the Sacrament of Confession," Catholic Online, uploaded April 26, 2016, http://www.catholic.org/prayers/prayer.php?p=1778.

28. "Protestantism and Roman Catholicism Compared: Penance," Roman Catholic Teachings, undated, http://www.romancatholicteachings.com/catholic_religion/penance.html.

28. Father Michael Azkoul, "What Are the Differences between Orthodoxy and Roman Catholicism?," Orthodox Christian Page, 1994, http://www.ocf.org/OrthodoxPage/reading/ortho_cath.html.

29. Richard A. Muller, *Calvin and the Reformed Tradition: On the Work of Christ and the Order of Salvation* (Grand Rapids, Michigan: Baker Publishing Group, 2012), 59–60.

29. John Calvin, *Institutio Christianae religionis*, tr. Henry Beveridge (Grand Rapids, Michigan: Wm. B. Eerdmans Publishing Company, 1989 [Latin orig. 1564]), Book III, Chapter 21: "Of the Eternal Election, by Which God Has Predestined Some to Salvation, and Others to Destruction," reposted to the Christian Classics Ethereal Library, June 1, 2005, at http://www.ccel.org/ccel/calvin/institutes.v.xxii.html.

30. Jonathan Edwards, "Sinners in the Hands of an Angry God" [1741], *The Works of President Edwards*, Vol. 6 (1817; New York: Burt Franklin, 1968), 458–62, ex-

cerpted online at http://www.wwnorton.com/college/history/archive/resourc-es/documents/ch03_03.htm.

31. "[B]ishops and priests, by virtue of the sacrament of Holy Orders, have the power to forgive all sins 'in the name of the Father, and of the Son, and of the Holy Spirit.' Forgiveness of sins brings reconciliation with God, but also with the Church. Since ancient times the bishop, visible head of a particular Church, has thus rightfully been considered to be the one who principally has the power and ministry of reconciliation: he is the moderator of the penitential discipline." "Catechism of the Catholic Church: Part Two—The Celebration of the Christian Mystery, Section Two—The Seven Sacraments of the Church, Chapter Two—The Sacraments of Healing."

32. Bruce Gerencser, "The Christian Get Out of Jail Free Card," Life and Times of Bruce Gerencser, June 7, 2015, https://brucegerencser.net/2015/06/the-chris-tian-get-out-of-jail-free-card/.

32. Quoted in Timothy Egan, "The End of Catholic Guilt," New York Times, April 15, 2016, https://www.nytimes.com/2016/04/15/opinion/the-end-of-catholic-guilt.html.

33. Quoted in Janet McCabe and Kim Akass, "What has Carmela Ever Done for Feminism?: Carmela Soprano and the Post-Feminist Dilemma," Reading the Sopranos: Hit TV from HBO, ed. David Lavery (New York: I.B. Tauris & Co, 2006), 39–55 [47].
    Interestingly David Chase, creator of The Sopranos, was not Catholic. He was an Italian-American Protestant. Robert Lloyd, "Mob Rules: David Chase on The Sopranos, the Small Screen, and Rock & Roll," LA Weekly, March 22, 2001, reposted at Robert Lloyd's website, House of Here, 2011, http://www.houseof-here.com/Weekly/davidchase01.html.

34. Donald DeMarco, "The Virtue of Compassion," Lay Witness (January–Feb-ruary 1999), reposted at the Catholic Education Resource Center, 2000, at http://www.catholiceducation.org/en/culture/catholic-contributions/the-vir-tue-of-compassion.html.

35. Quoted in James Carroll, "The Holocaust and the Catholic Church," Atlantic, October 1999, https://www.theatlantic.com/magazine/archive/1999/10/the-ho-locaust-and-the-catholic-church/305061.

36. Galileo probably never actually uttered that famous line after his conviction. But it is true that he never stopped believing that the Earth revolves around the sun. Jessica Wolf, "The Truth about Galileo and His Conflict with the Cath-olic Church," UCLA Newsroom, December 22, 2016, http://newsroom.ucla.edu/releases/the-truth-about-galileo-and-his-conflict-with-the-catholic-church.

38. Alan Cowell, "After 350 Years, Vatican Says Galileo was Right: It Moves," *New York Times*, October 31, 1992, http://www.nytimes.com/1992/10/31/world/after-350-years-vatican-says-galileo-was-right-it-moves.html.

    Many believe that Copernicus, another scientist distinguished for his pioneering views on heliocentricity, deserves an apology too, but he actually maintained an excellent relationship with the Catholic Church throughout his life. Steph Solis, "Copernicus and the Church: What the History Books Don't Say," *Christian Science Monitor*, February 19, 2013, http://www.csmonitor.com/Technology/2013/0219/Copernicus-and-the-Church-What-the-history-books-don-t-say.

39. Stephen Jay Gould, "Nonoverlapping Magisteria," *Natural History*, 106 (March 1997), 16–22 [22].

40. Quoted in Nick Pisa, "Pope Benedict Faces New Criticism on Sexual Abuse Record," *Telegraph*, March 21, 2010, http://www.telegraph.co.uk/news/world-news/europe/ireland/7494539/Pope-Benedict-faces-new-criticism-on-sexu-al-abuse-record.html. Pope Benedict was citing John 8:7.

41. "Council of Trent," *Encyclopædia Britannica*, July 20, 1998, last updated April 26, 2016, https://www.britannica.com/event/Council-of-Trent.

    Indulgences were part of a complicated medieval system used to measure sins versus levels of forgiveness. Indulgences were applied toward penance, and could be issued by church officials. Luther protested that the sale of indulgences was corrupt, and the Catholic Church, fifty years later, conceded the point. Lawrence G. Duggan, "Indulgence," *Encyclopædia Britannica*, July 20, 1998, last updated November 25, 2015, https://www.britannica.com/topic/indulgence.

45. "The 21 Ecumenical Councils," New Advent, 2007, http://www.newadvent.org/library/almanac_14388a.htm.

46. Quoted in Jordan G. Teicher, "Why Is Vatican II So Important?" NPR, October 10, 2012, http://www.npr.org/2012/10/10/162573716/why-is-vatican-ii-so-important.

46. Maureen Fiedler, "Vatican II: It's About That 'Fresh Air,'" *National Catholic Reporter*, October 8, 2012, https://www.ncronline.org/blogs/ncr-today/vatican-ii-its-about-fresh-air.

47. Eileen Marie, "Divorce Prior to Vatican II," and Reverend Mark J. Gantley, "Answer," EWTN Global Catholic Network, September 15–16, 2004, http://www.ewtn.com/v/experts/showmessage.asp?number=411602.

48. Quoted in Teicher, "Why Is Vatican II So Important?"

49. Alan Wolfe, *The Transformation of American Religion: How We Actually Live Our Faith* (Chicago: University of Chicago Press, 2005), 172.

50. Luke 18:25.

51. Cathy Lynn Grossman, Religious News Service, "Christ, Marx, and Che: Fidel Castro Offers Pope His Religious Views," *National Catholic Reporter*, September 21, 2015, https://www.ncronline.org/news/world/christ-marx-and-che-fidel-castro-offers-pope-his-religious-views.

51. Cf. Mehdi Hasan, "Jesus was a Lefty," *New Statesman*, December 15, 2010, http://www.newstatesman.com/religion/2010/12/jesus-god-tax-christ-health.

52. John Dear, "Gustavo Gutierrez and the Preferential Option for the Poor," *National Catholic Reporter*, November 8, 2011, https://www.ncronline.org/blogs/road-peace/gustavo-gutierrez-and-preferential-option-poor.

52. Book II. The People of God Liber II. De Populo Dei, Part I. The Christian Faithful, Title I. The Obligations and Rights of All the Christian Faithful, Holy See, undated, http://www.vatican.va/archive/ENG1104/__PU.HTM.

53. John Cassidy, "The Disastrous Influence of Pope Benedict XVI," *New Yorker*, February 12, 2013, http://www.newyorker.com/news/john-cassidy/the-disastrous-influence-of-pope-benedict-xvi.

57. "Year of the Three Popes," from the feature "The Pontificate of Pope John Paul II," EWTN Global Catholic Network, undated, https://www.ewtn.com/johnpaul2/life/1978.htm.

57. Filip Mazurczak, "How Saint John Paul II Conquered Communism," Catholic World Report, June 16, 2016, http://www.catholicworldreport.com/Item/4850/how_saint_john_paul_ii_conquered_communism.aspx.

57. Ranald Macaulay, "The Counter-Reformation of Pope John Paul II," Jubilee Centre, September 2000, http://www.jubilee-centre.org/the-counter-reformation-of-pope-john-paul-ii-by-ranald-macaulay/

57. Pope Paul II, "Homily of His Holiness John Paul II," Holy See, October 8, 1995, https://w2.vatican.va/content/john-paul-ii/en/homilies/1995/documents/hf_jp-ii_hom_19951008_baltimore.html..

58. Quoted in Marius Heuser and Peter Schwarz, "Pope John Paul II: A Political Obituary," World Socialist Web Site, April 6, 2005, https://www.wsws.org/en/articles/2005/04/pope-a06.html.

59. Craig Shirley, "Another President, Another Pope," *U.S. News & World Report*, September 24, 2015, https://www.usnews.com/opinion/articles/2015/09/24/ronald-reagan-pope-john-paul-ii-and-the-alliance-that-won-the-cold-war.

59. Gerald Posner interview with NPR Staff, "From Laundering to Profiteering, a Multitude of Sins at the Vatican Bank," NPR, January 30, 2015, http://www.npr.org/2015/01/30/382374060/from-laundering-to-profiteering-a-multitude-of-sins-at-the-vatican-bank.

60. Sabrina Arena Ferrisi, "John Paul II Meets Vatican II," Legatus, May 1, 2010, http://legatus.org/john-paul-ii-meets-vatican-ii/.

61. "John Paul II in His Own Words," BBC, October 14, 2003, http://news.bbc.co.uk/2/hi/europe/3112868.stm.

61. Joel Roberts, "John Paul's Conservative Legacy," CBS News, April 3, 2005, http://www.cbsnews.com/news/john-pauls-conservative-legacy/.

61. Bevil Bramwell, "Only the Chaste," The Catholic Thing, May 3, 2015, https://www.thecatholicthing.org/2015/05/03/only-the-chaste/.

62. Catherine Kroeger, "The Neglected History of Women in the Early Church," Christian History, 17 (1988), reposted to the Christianity Today website in May 2017, at http://www.christianitytoday.com/history/issues/issue-17/neglected-history-of-women-in-early-church.html.

63. John Paul II, "Apostolic Letter Ordinatio Sacerdotalis of John Paul II to the Bishops of the Catholic Church on Reserving Priestly Ordination to Men Alone," Holy See, May 22, 1994, http://w2.vatican.va/content/john-paul-ii/en/apost_letters/1994/documents/hf_jp-ii_apl_19940522_ordinatio-sacerdotalis.html.

64. Samuel Gregg, "Dissenting Catholics' Modernity Problem," Crisis Magazine, October 28, 2011, http://www.crisismagazine.com/2011/dissenting-catholics-modernity-problem.

64. Stephen Bates, "Condoms and the Catholic Church: A Short History," Guardian, November 21, 2010, https://www.theguardian.com/world/2010/nov/21/condoms-birth-control-catholic-church-short-history.

64. Quoted in Elisabeth Rosenthal, "Top Catholics Question Condom Ban," New York Times, April 16, 2005, http://www.nytimes.com/2005/04/16/world/europe/top-catholics-question-condom-ban.html.

65. "The Vatican's Child Abuse Response," BBC News, April 11, 2014, http://www.bbc.com/news/world-europe-25757218.

66. Jason Berry, "The Shame of John Paul II: How the Sex Abuse Scandal Stained His Papacy," Nation, April 27, 2011, https://www.thenation.com/article/shame-john-paul-ii-how-sex-abuse-scandal-stained-his-papacy/.

66. Quoted in ibid.

67. Madeleine Baran, "Betrayed by Silence: A Story in Four Chapters," Chapter 2: "The Church Protects Its Own," Minnesota Public Radio, July 21, 2014, http://minnesota.publicradio.org/collections/catholic-church/betrayed-by-silence/ch2.

67. Michael Powell and Lois Romano, "Roman Catholic Church Shifts Legal Strategy," Washington Post, May 13, 2002, updated May 15, 2002, https://www.washingtonpost.com/archive/politics/2002/05/13/roman-catholic-church-shifts-legal-strategy/49c1ce20-82e0-41f8-a750-ebb1c05d8ca6/.

67. Dan Merica, "7 Reasons Catholics Leave Church (in Trenton, #1 Is Sex Abuse Crisis," *Belief* blog, CNN, March 30, 2012, http://religion.blogs.cnn.com/2012/03/30/7-reasons-catholics-leave-church-in-trenton-1-is-sex-abuse-crisis.

68. Catherine Pepinster, "The Dark Box: A Secret History of Confession by John Cornwell—Review," *Observer*, February 23, 2014, https://www.theguardian.com/books/2014/feb/23/dark-box-john-cornwell-review.

68. John Cornwell, *The Dark Box: A Secret History of Confession* (New York: Basic Books, 2014).

68. Ibid.

69. Alma Guillermoprieto, "Francis's Holy War: How This Charismatic, Radical Pope Keeps Surprising the World—While Secretly Dividing the Catholic Church," *Matter*, June 23, 2014, https://medium.com/matter/franciss-holy-war-70a382606c0d.

69. Dan Delzell, "Why Priests Should Be Allowed to Marry," *Christian Post*, September 22, 2013, http://www.christianpost.com/news/why-priests-should-be-allowed-to-marry-104631/.

70. Reposted online at Bible Gateway, undated, at https://www.biblegateway.com/passage/?search=1%20Corinthians%207:25-40.

70. "Pope Seeks to Clarify Reasons for Celibacy," *New York Times*, July 18, 1993, http://www.nytimes.com/1993/07/18/world/pope-seeks-to-clarify-reasons-for-celibacy.html.

   Chastity, in fact, was not universal for priests until the sixteenth century. Guillermoprieto, "Francis's Holy War."

71. Thomas G. Plante, "Six Important Points You Don't Hear About Regarding Clergy Sexual Abuse in the Catholic Church," *Psychology Today*, March 24, 2010, https://www.psychologytoday.com/blog/do-the-right-thing/201003/six-important-points-you-dont-hear-about-regarding-clergy-sexual.

71. Ibid. Though of course it's important to note that statistics on childhood sexual abuse are exceptionally difficult to determine, as they often depend upon the victims' self-reporting, experts agree that the incidence is far greater than what is reported to authorities. "Child Sexual Abuse Statistics," National Center for Victims of Crime, 2012, https://victimsofcrime.org/media/reporting-on-child-sexual-abuse/child-sexual-abuse-statistics.

73. Bill Tammeus, "Episcopal Church Celebrates 40 Years of Women in the Priesthood," *National Catholic Reporter*, July 28, 2014, https://www.ncronline.org/news/faith-parish/episcopal-church-celebrates-40-years-women-priesthood.

78. Peter Ford, "Europe Cringes at Bush's 'Crusade' against Terrorists," *Christian Science Monitor*, September 19, 2001, http://www.csmonitor.com/2001/0919/p12s2-woeu.html.

78. Dexter Filkins, *The Forever War* (New York: Alfred A. Knopf, 2008).

78. Robert Fisk, *The Great War for Civilisation: The Conquest of the Middle East* (London: Fourth Estate, 2005).

78. Peter Ford, "Europe Cringes at Bush 'Crusade' Against Terrorists," *Christian Science Monitor*, September 19, 2001, https://www.csmonitor.com/2001/0919/p12s2-woeu.html.

79. Eyder Peralta, "'Torture Report': A Closer Look at When and What President Bush Knew," NPR, December 16, 2014, http://www.npr.org/sections/thetwo-way/2014/12/16/369876047/torture-report-a-closer-look-at-when-and-what-president-bush-knew.

79. David Gow, "Bush Gives Green Light to CIA for Assassination of Named Terrorists," *Guardian*, October 28, 2001, https://www.theguardian.com/world/2001/oct/29/afghanistan.terrorism3.

79. Severin Carrell, "The Children of Guantanamo Bay," *Independent*, May 27, 2006, http://www.independent.co.uk/news/world/americas/the-children-of-guantanamo-bay-480059.html.

79. Cory Doctorow, "Memoir of a Child Kidnapped to Guantanamo Bay, Tortured for Six Years, and Released," Boing Boing, December 14, 2011, http://boingboing.net/2011/12/14/memoir-of-a-child-kidnapped-to.html.

80. Dana Milbank, "Pope Presses Bush on Iraq Violence," *Washington Post*, June 5, 2005, A1, http://www.washingtonpost.com/wp-dyn/articles/A14823-2004Jun4.html.

80. Frank Bruni, "Threats and Responses: The Vatican; Pope Voices Opposition, His Strongest, to Iraq War," *New York Times*, January 14, 2003, http://www.nytimes.com/2003/01/14/world/threats-responses-vatican-pope-voices-opposition-his-strongest-iraq-war.html.

81. J.Y. Smith, "The Church Loses Its Light," *Washington Post*, April 3, 2005, A31, http://www.washingtonpost.com/wp-dyn/articles/A21187-2005Apr2.html.

82. Quoted in Associated Press, "'Let Me Go to the House of the Father': Pope John Paul II's Last Words Detailed in Vatican Report," NBC News, September 17, 2005, http://www.nbcnews.com/id/9377134/ns/world_news-europe/t/let-me-go-house-father.

82. "The Riddle of John Paul II," Beliefnet, undated, http://www.beliefnet.com/faiths/2000/02/the-riddle-of-john-paul-ii.aspx.

83. Slavoj Žižek, "The Popes Failures," *In These Times*, April 8, 2005, http://inthese-times.com/article/2059.

84. Richard N. Ostling, "Catholics Looking for Reform Likely to Be Disappointed," *Daily Herald*, April 10, 2005, http://www.heraldextra.com/news/world/catho-lics-looking-for-reform-likely-to-be-disappointed/article_acd74a51-6584-5492-9f4e-15311f2614a5.html.

85. Ian Fisher, "German Cardinal Is Chosen as Pope," *New York Times*, April 20, 2005, http://www.nytimes.com/2005/04/20/world/worldspecial2/german-cardi-nal-is-chosen-as-pope.html.

89. "Pope Benedict XVI Reflects on Life Under Hitler's Nazi Party," Catholic On-line, May 31, 2011, http://www.catholic.org/news/international/europe/story.php?id=41597.

89. Susan Donaldson James, "Pope Benedict Dogged by Hitler Youth Past, Despite Jewish Support," ABC News, February 12, 2013, http://abcnews.go.com/In-ternational/pope-benedict-dogged-nazi-past-achievements-jewish-relations/story?id=18469350.

89. Stephen Bates and John Hooper, "From Hitler Youth to the Vatican," *Guardian*, April 20, 2005, https://www.theguardian.com/world/2005/apr/20/catholicism.religion3.

90. Quoted in Joshua J. McElwee, "Benedict Says He Did Not Expect Papacy, Ac-cepted It as Duty to Cardinals," *National Catholic Reporter*, September 9, 2016, https://www.ncronline.org/news/vatican/benedict-says-he-did-not-expect-papa-cy-accepted-it-duty-cardinals.

90. Trisha Bee and Cary Docter, "Too Tired to Go On, Pope Benedict XVI to Resign on February 28th," Fox 6 Now, February 11, 2013, http://fox6now.com/2013/02/11/pope-benedict-to-resign-at-the-end-of-the-month-vatican-says/amp.

91. Quoted in Lizzy Davies, John Hooper, and Kate Connolly, "Pope Benedict XVI Resigns Owing to Age and Declining Health," *Guardian*, February 11, 2013, https://www.theguardian.com/world/2013/feb/11/pope-benedict-xvi-resigns-age.

91. Quoted in ibid.

91. San Martín, "Benedict Says He Quit Because He Couldn't Face Another Trip."

92. Walter Russell Mead, "Benedict's Choice and the Crisis of the Western Church," American Interest, February 24, 2013, https://www.the-american-in-terest.com/2013/02/24/benedicts-choice-and-the-crisis-of-the-western-church.

92. Bee and Docter, "Too Tired to Go On."

93. Ibid.

93. Quoted in Ian Traynor, Karen McVeigh, and Henry McDonald, "Pope Benedict 'Complicit in Child Sex Abuse Scandals,' Say Victims' Groups," *Guardian*, February 11, 2013, https://www.theguardian.com/world/2013/feb/11/pope-complicit-child-abuse-say-victims.

94. Quoted in ibid.

95. Stephen Bates, "Pope Benedict XVI Oversaw Church Drift into Conservative Authoritarianism," *Guardian*, February 11, 2013, https://www.theguardian.com/world/2013/feb/11/pope-drift-conservative-authoritarian.

96. Quoted in ibid.

97. Quoted in Cassidy, "Disastrous Influence of Pope Benedict XVI."

98. Tom Peters, "Under Promise, Over Deliver," Tom Peters, 1987, http://tompeters.com/columns/under-promise-over-deliver/.

101. Manya A. Brachear, "Cardinal George Surprised by the Choice—and the Name," *Chicago Tribune*, March 14, 2013, http://articles.chicagotribune.com/2013-03-14/news/ct-met-cardinal-george-pope-picked-0314-20130314_1_cardinal-george-pope-francis-sistine-chapel.

101. Paulo Prada and Helen Popper, "Special Report: Behind the Charm, a Political Pope," Reuters, March 27, 2013, http://www.reuters.com/article/us-pope-profile-specialreport-idUSBRE92Q09P20130327.

102. John L. Allen Jr., "Profile: New Pope, Jesuit Bergoglio, was Runner-Up in 2005 Conclave," *National Catholic Reporter*, March 3, 2013, https://www.ncronline.org/blogs/ncr-today/papabile-day-men-who-could-be-pope-13.

103. David Gibson, "The Story behind Pope Francis' Election," *USA Today*, March 16, 2013, https://www.usatoday.com/story/news/world/2013/03/16/pope-francis-election-conclave/1992797.

103. Ross Douthat, "Will Pope Francis Break the Church?" *Atlantic*, May 2015, https://www.theatlantic.com/magazine/archive/2015/05/will-pope-francis-break-the-church/389516.

104. Gerald Posner interview with NPR Staff, "From Laundering to Profiteering."

105. Ibid.

105. Eileen P. Flynn, "The Vatican Bank Scandal Nobody Is Talking About," *America: The Jesuit Review*, July 15, 2015, https://www.americamagazine.org/content/all-things/vatican-bank-scandal-nobody-talking-about.

105. Gerald Posner interview with NPR Staff, "From Laundering to Profiteering."

106. Ibid.

108. Gibson, "Story behind Pope Francis' Election."

108. Philip Jenkins, "Catholicism's Incredible Growth Story," *Catholic Herald*, September 8, 2016, http://www.catholicherald.co.uk/issues/september-9th-2016/catholicisms-incredible-growth-story/.

109. Gibson, "Story behind Pope Francis' Election."

110. Quoted in ibid.

111. Quoted in ibid.

112. Quoted in ibid.

115. Quoted in "Pope Francis Reveals Why He Chose His Name," *Catholic Herald*, March 16, 2013, http://www.catholicherald.co.uk/news/2013/03/16/pope-francis-reveals-why-he-chose-name.

116. Jim Yardley, "A Humble Pope, Challenging the World," *New York Times*, September 18, 2015, https://www.nytimes.com/2015/09/19/world/europe/pope-francis.html.

116. "John 13:1–17 New International Version (NIV): Jesus Washes His Disciples' Feet," Bible Gateway, undated, https://www.biblegateway.com/passage/?search=John%2013:1-17.

116. Alessandro Speciale, "Pope Washes Feet of Two Girls, Two Muslims, at Youth Prison," *Washington Post*, March 28, 2013, https://www.washingtonpost.com/national/on-faith/pope-washes-feet-of-two-girls-two-muslims-at-youth-prison/2013/03/28/0a7c573e-97e5-11e2-b5b4-b63027b499de_story.html.

117. Laurie Goodstein, "Vatican Ends Battle with U.S. Catholic Nuns' Group," *New York Times*, April 16, 2015, https://www.nytimes.com/2015/04/17/us/catholic-church-ends-takeover-of-leadership-conference-of-women-religious.html.

117. "Congregation for the Doctrine of the Faith Concludes Mandate Regarding LCWR," Leadership Conference of Women Religious, April 13–16, 2015, https://lcwr.org/media/news/congregation-doctrine-faith-concludes-mandate-regarding-lcwr.

118. Robert Hennelly, "How Pope Francis Turned Around Troubled Vatican Bank," *MoneyWatch*, CBS News, September 25, 2015, http://www.cbsnews.com/news/how-pope-francis-turned-around-troubled-vatican-bank.

118. Gregg Fields, "One Holy Mess: Pope Francis Fights Institutional Corruption at the Vatican Bank," Edmond J. Safra Center for Ethics, Harvard University, August 22, 2013, https://ethics.harvard.edu/blog/one-holy-mess.

118. "Pope Francis Replaces Four Cardinals on Vatican Bank Commission," Catholic Online, January 17, 2014, http://www.catholic.org/news/international/europe/story.php?id=53912.

118. Quoted in Robert Hennelly, "How Pope Francis Turned Around Troubled Vatican Bank."

119. Quoted in Rachel Donadio, "On Gay Priests, Pope Francis Asks, 'Who Am I to Judge?'" *New York Times*, July 29, 2013, http://www.nytimes.com/2013/07/30/world/europe/pope-francis-gay-priests.html.

120. Quoted in ibid.

121. Quoted in ibid.

122. Quoted in ibid.

123. Laurie Goodstein, "Pope Says Church is 'Obsessed' with Gays, Abortion and Birth Control," *New York Times*, September 19, 2013, http://www.nytimes.com/2013/09/20/world/europe/pope-bluntly-faults-churchs-focus-on-gays-and-abortion.html.

124. Quoted in ibid.

125. Quoted in ibid.

126. Pope Francis, *Amoris Lætitia* (The Joy of Love), Holy See, March 19, 2016, https://w2.vatican.va/content/dam/francesco/pdf/apost_exhortations/documents/papa-francesco_esortazione-ap_20160319_amoris-laetitia_en.pdf.

127. Ibid. Francis is here quoting from the report delivered to him by the synod of bishops convened the previous year—"Relatio Finalis," Holy See, October 24, 2015, http://www.vatican.va/roman_curia/synod/documents/rc_synod_doc_20151026_relazione-finale-xiv-assemblea_en.html.

127. Megan Sweas, "Pope Francis' New 'Joy of Love' Exhortation Won't Resolve Catholic Tensions on Marriage and Sex," *Los Angeles Times*, April 12, 2016, http://www.latimes.com/opinion/op-ed/la-oe-sweas-pope-joy-of-love-catholic--20160412-story.html.

129. Quoted in "Pope Apologises to Victims of Clerical Sexual Abuse," *La Stampa*, July 7, 2014, http://www.lastampa.it/2014/07/07/vaticaninsider/eng/the-vatican/pope-apologises-to-victims-of-clerical-sexual-abuse-558S6etttB2iGtrWgbgfzK/amphtml/pagina.amp.html.

130. Quoted in "Pope: 'No Place' in the Church for Those Who Commit Sexual Abuse," AsiaNews, July 7, 2014, http://www.asianews.it/news-en/Pope:-no-place-in-the-Church-for-those-who-commit-sexual-abuse-31558.html.

130. Quoted in Jim Yardley, "Pope Asks Forgiveness from Victims of Sex Abuse," *New York Times*, July 7, 2014, https://www.nytimes.com/2014/07/08/world/europe/pope-francis-begs-forgiveness-of-victims-of-sex-abuse.html.

131. Quoted in Edward Pentin, "Synod's Final Report Lacks Bishops' Consensus on Controversial Topics," *National Catholic Register*, October 18, 2014, http://www.ncregister.com/blog/edward-pentin/synods-final-document-lacks-bishops-consensus-on-controversial-topics.

131. Ibid.

132. Dorothy Cummings McLean, "Pope Francis Names Pro-LGBT Priest as Auxiliary Bishop in San Diego," LifeSiteNews, May 29, 2017, https://www.lifesitenews.com/news/pope-francis-names-pro-lgbt-priest-as-auxiliary-bishop-in-san-diego.

133. "Great Schism," New World Encyclopedia, July 14, 2017, http://www.newworldencyclopedia.org/entry/Great_Schism.

133. Quoted in Gerard O'Connell, "Pope Assures Orthodox: We Want Unity, Not Assimilation or Submission," *America: The Jesuit Review*, November 30, 2014, http://www.americamagazine.org/content/dispatches/pope-assures-orthodox-we-want-unity-not-assimilation-or-submission.

135. David Gibson, "U.S. Cardinal Raymond Burke: Pope Francis Opposes Abortion and Gay Marriage," *Washington Post*, February 21, 2014, https://www.washingtonpost.com/local/us-cardinal-raymond-burke-pope-francis-opposes-abortion-and-gay-marriage/2014/02/21/de5dbf52-9b36-11e3-975d-107dfef7b668_story.html.

135. Mark Memmott, "Pope Oks Communion for the Divorced? Not So Fast, Vatican Says," NPR, April 24, 2014, https://www.npr.org/sections/thetwo-way/2014/04/24/306515332/pope-oks-communion-for-the-divorced-not-so-fast-vatican-says.

139. Yardley, "A Humble Pope, Challenging the World."

139. "Biography of the Holy Father Francis," Holy See, undated, http://w2.vatican.va/content/francesco/en/biography/documents/papa-francesco-biografia-bergoglio.html.

139. John L. Allen Jr., "Pope's Family Story Fuels His Passion for Immigrants and the Poor," Crux, May 10, 2015, https://cruxnow.com/church/2015/05/10/popes-family-story-fuels-his-passion-for-immigrants-and-the-poor/.

140. Departamento de Derecho y Ciencias Políticas, Universidad Nacional de La Matanza, "Historias de inmigrantes italianos en Argentina," Argentina Investiga, November 14, 2011, http://argentinainvestiga.edu.ar/noticia.php?titulo=historias_de_inmigrantes_italianos_en_argentina&id=1432#.U2cKkYHa70s.

140. Samuel L. Baily, *Immigrants in the Lands of Promise: Italians in Buenos Aires and New York City, 1870–1914* (Ithaca, New York: Cornell University Press, 1999), 54.

140. Michael T. Luongo, "Exploring the Homeland of Pope Francis I," *New York Times*, May 9, 2013, http://www.nytimes.com/2013/05/12/travel/exploring-the-homeland-of-pope-francis-i.html.

140. Claudio Iván Remeseira, "Pope Francis: A Humble and Outspoken Man, and Technically Also Italian," NBC Latino, March 14, 2013, http://nbclatino.

com/2013/03/14/pope-francis-a-humble-and-outspoken-man-and-technically-also-italian/.

140. Austen Ivereigh, *The Great Reformer: Francis and the Making of a Radical Pope* (New York: Henry Holt and Company, 2014), 17.

141. Ibid., 13–16.

141. Ibid., 17.

142. Mark K. Shriver, "6 Childhood Experiences That Defined Pope Francis," *Time*, November 15, 2016, http://time.com/4543112/pilgrimage-pope-francis.

143. Daniel K. Lewis, *The History of Argentina* (New York: St. Martin's Griffin, 2003), 93–105.

144. Roberto Bosca, "Una excomunión que no se cumplió," *La Nacion*, December 2, 2001, http://www.lanacion.com.ar/210497-unaexcomunion-que-no-se-cumplio.

145. Quoted in Ivereigh, *Great Reformer*, 25.

145. Ibid., 35–36.

146. Quoted in Sean Salai, SJ, *What Would Pope Francis Do?: Bringing the Good News to People in Need* (Huntington, Indiana: Our Sunday Visitor, 2016), 53.

147. Quoted in Ivereigh, *Great Reformer*, 31.

148. Francesca Ambrogetti and Sergio Rubín, *Pope Francis: His Life in His Own Words—Conversations with Jorge Bergoglio* (New York: G.P. Putnam's Sons, 2013), 13.

148. Sergio Rubín, "El Papa argentino," *Clarín*, Suplemento Especial: "El Papa del fin del mundo," March 17, 2013, 4–8 [8], http://contenidos2.clarin.com/edicion-electronica/20130317/index.html#/8/.

148. Alex Knapp, "Pope Francis, Scientist," *Forbes*, March 12, 2013, https://www.forbes.com/sites/alexknapp/2013/03/12/pope-francis-scientist-2/#35a76cdf4486.

148. Ibid.

148. Courtney Walsh, "Pope Francis Reveals He Used to Work as a Bar Bouncer," *Fox News*, December 3, 2013, http://www.foxnews.com/world/2013/12/03/pope-francis-reveals-used-to-work-as-bouncer.html.

149. Matt Roper, "High School Friends of Pope Francis Reveal How the Young Pontiff Fell Head Over Heels in Love with a Beautiful Brunette, Held 'Unforgettable' Parties and Pranked His High School Teachers," *Daily Mail*, March 14, 2015, updated March 16, 2015, http://www.dailymail.co.uk/news/article-2979533/EXCLUSIVE-Pope-10-Muchachos-Friends-reveal-young-pontiff-fell-head-heels-love-beautiful-brunette-held-unforgettable-parties-pranked-high-school-teachers.html.

149. "Bergoglio, sobre todo 'pastor,' tanguero y simpatizante de San Lorenzo," Agencia Informativa Católica Argentina, March 13, 2013, http://www.aica.org/5517-bergoglio-sobre-todo-pastor-tanguero-simpatizante-de-san-lorenzo.html.

149. Quoted in Ivereigh, *Great Reformer*, 36.

150. "Bergoglio, sobre todo 'pastor,' tanguero y simpatizante de San Lorenzo."

150. Lewis, *History of Argentina*, 114.

150. Ivereigh, *Great Reformer*, 30.

151. "Pope Francis," ReligionFacts, November 22, 2016, http://www.religionfacts.com/pope-francis.

151. "En 1958, Bergoglio hizo su noviciado en Chile," *La Segunda*, March 13, 2013, http://www.lasegunda.com/Noticias/Nacional/2013/03/829934/En-1958-Bergoglio-hizo-su-noviciado-en-Chile.

151. Ivereigh, *Great Reformer*, 48.

152. Michael Warren, "Pope Francis Still Has Most of His Right Lung," *U.S. News & World Report*, April 1, 2013, https://www.usnews.com/news/world/articles/2013/04/01/pope-francis-still-has-most-of-his-right-lung.

152. John L. Allen, *The Francis Miracle: Inside the Transformation of the Pope and the Church* (New York: Time Home Entertainment, 2015), 16.

153. Ivereigh, *Great Reformer*, 48.

153. Quoted in ibid.

154. Ibid., 56.

154. Ivereigh, *Great Reformer*, 57.

155. "Biography of the Holy Father Francis," Holy See.

155. Ivereigh, *Great Reformer*, 79.

155. Ibid.

155. "Pope Francis," ReligionFacts.

156. Quoted in Ivereigh, *Great Reformer*, 80.

157. Quoted in ibid., 95.

158. Ibid., 108–09.

158. Quoted in Joyce Hackel, "Was Pope Francis Silent during Argentina's Dirty War?" PRI (Public Radio International), September 23, 2015, https://www.pri.org/stories/2015-09-23/was-pope-francis-silent-during-argentinas-dirty-war.

159. Quoted in David Gibson, "To Understand Pope Francis, Look to the Jesuits," *National Catholic Reporter*, March 12, 2014, https://www.ncronline.org/news/vatican/understand-pope-francis-look-jesuits.

159. "Dirty War," *Encyclopædia Britannica*, November 12, 2009, last updated March 20, 2014, https://www.britannica.com/event/Dirty-War.

160. For example, Bishop Enrique Angelelli was killed in a traffic accident in 1976 while carrying evidence about two murdered priests. Bergoglio became cardinal of Buenos Aires in 2001 but waited five years, until the then-president declared an official day of mourning for Angelelli, before declaring him a "martyr." It was the first time the church acknowledged that Angelelli had been murdered. Associated Press, "Election of Pope Francis Stirs Argentina's 'Dirty War' Past, and Role of Church in Deaths of Thousands," *National Post*, March 14, 2013, http://news.nationalpost.com/news/election-of-pope-francis-stirs-argentinas-dirty-war-past-and-role-of-church-in-deaths-of-thousands.

160. Quoted in ibid.

163. Quoted in Guillermoprieto, "Francis's Holy War."

164. Ivereigh, *Great Reformer*, 133–34.

166. Ibid., 133–35.

167. Ibid.

168. Jon Lee Anderson, "Pope Francis and the Dirty War," *New Yorker*, March 14, 2013, http://www.newyorker.com/news/daily-comment/pope-francis-and-the-dirty-war.

169. Guillermoprieto, "Francis's Holy War."

169. Quoted in ibid.

170. Ivereigh, *Great Reformer*, 117.

171. Guillermoprieto, "Francis's Holy War."

171. Hackel, "Was Pope Francis Silent during Argentina's Dirty War?"

172. Quoted in Hackel, "Was Pope Francis Silent during Argentina's Dirty War?"

172. Guillermoprieto, "Francis's Holy War."

172. Quoted in Associated Press, "Election of Pope Francis Stirs Argentina's 'Dirty War' Past."

173. Quoted in Silvina Frydlewsky and Anthony Faiola, "Bergoglio Challenged Moral Authority of Argentina's Elected Leaders," *Washington Post*, March 14, 2013, https://www.washingtonpost.com/world/the_americas/bergoglio-challenged-moral-authority-of-argentinas-elected-leaders/2013/03/14/95db94f6-8ce7-11e2-b63f-f53fb9f2fcb4_story.html.

174. Paul Vallely, *Pope Francis: Untying the Knots—The Struggle for the Soul of Catholicism* (London: Bloomsbury, 2015), 80.

174. Guillermoprieto, "Francis's Holy War."

175. Chris Millington, "Vichy France, Collaboration and Resistance," FrenchHistoryOnline, 2012, https://frenchhistoryonline.com/vichy-france-and-the-second-word-war/vichy-france-collaboration-and-resistance-a-lecture-by-chris-millington/.

175. Guillermoprieto, "Francis's Holy War."

175. Associated Press, "Election of Pope Francis Stirs Argentina's 'Dirty War' Past."

176. Quoted in ibid.

177. Quoted in ibid.

178. Ibid.

178. Quoted in ibid.

179. Jimmy Burns, *Francis, Pope of Good Promise* (New York: St. Martin's Press, 2015), 181–82.

179. Lewis, *History of Argentina*, 149–50.

179. Guillermoprieto, "Francis's Holy War."

180. Vallely, *Pope Francis: Untying the Knots*, 58–60.

180. Ivereigh, *Great Reformer*, 202–04.

181. Ibid., 110.

181. Veronica Stracqualursi, "Pope Francis: Where He Learned to Speak English," ABC News, September 23, 2015, http://abcnews.go.com/US/pope-francis-learned-speak-english/story?id=33980170.

181. Ivereigh, *Great Reformer*, 197–98.

182. Fernando Montes, SJ, quoted in Ivereigh, *Great Reformer*, 194.

183. Quoted by Antonio Spadaro in Guillermoprieto, "Francis's Holy War."

184. Daniel Burke, "The Pope's Dark Night of the Soul," CNN, September 21, 2015, http://www.cnn.com/interactive/2015/09/specials/pope-dark-night-of-the-soul/.

185. Ivereigh, *Great Reformer*, 197.

186. Margaret Hebblethwaite, "The Pope Francis I Know," *Guardian*, March 14, 2013, https://www.theguardian.com/commentisfree/2013/mar/14/the-pope-francis-i-know.

187. Quoted in Barbie Latza Nadeau, "Pope Francis Tells Priests to Have Exorcists on Call," Daily Beast, March 19, 2017, http://www.thedailybeast.com/pope-francis-tells-priests-to-have-exorcists-on-call.

191. Gibson, "To Understand Pope Francis."

191. Quoted in ibid.

192. Quoted in ibid.

192. Quoted in ibid. The citation is of Matthew 21:42.

193. Quoted in Gibson, "To Understand Pope Francis."

193. "Days of Penance," *Economist*, August 22, 2013, https://www.economist.com/news/books-and-arts/21583979-hard-lessons-dark-time-days-penance.

194. Haley Cohen, "Slum Priests: Pope Francis's Early Years," *Atlantic*, March 20, 2013, https://www.theatlantic.com/international/archive/2013/03/slum-priests-pope-franciss-early-years/274201/.

194. Philip Pullella, "U.N. Should Encourage Redistribution of Wealth, Pope Says," *Chicago Tribune*, May 9, 2014, http://articles.chicagotribune.com/2014-05-09/features/sns-rt-us-pope-un-20140509_1_pope-francis-first-non-european-pope-united-nations.

194. Michael Daly, "Pope Francis Has Done Penance for His Lapse of Courage in Argentina," Daily Beast, March 19, 2013, http://www.thedailybeast.com/articles/2013/03/19/pope-francis-has-done-penance-for-his-lapse-of-courage-in-argentina.

196. "San Roberto Bellarmino (Cardinal Titular Church)," Catholic-Hierarchy, June 5, 2004, updated July 11, 2017, http://www.catholic-hierarchy.org/diocese/d1r04.html.

196. Jose Maria Poirier, "Quiet Thunder in Argentina," *Catholic Herald*, March 13, 2013, http://www.catholicherald.co.uk/news/2013/03/13/quiet-thunder-in-argentina/.

197. "Canonization: 4 Steps to Becoming a Saint," Sadlier We Believe Blog, April 2014, http://www.catholichawaii.org/media/314379/canonization_4_steps_to_becoming_a_saint.pdf.

197. Colin McMahon, "Sainthood Effort for 5 Slain Recalls Argentine 'Dirty War,'" *Chicago Tribune*, August 12, 2005, http://articles.chicagotribune.com/2005-08-12/news/0508120166_1_beatification-buenos-aires-argentine-dirty.

198. Allen, "Profile: New Pope, Jesuit Bergoglio."

198. Sergio Rubín, "'El Jesuita,' Biography of Jorge Bergoglio, Tells of Pope Francis' Humble Beginnings in the Church That He Maintained throughout His Cardinalship," *New York Daily News*, March 14, 2013, http://www.nydailynews.com/news/world/pope-francis-humble-affable-servant-article-1.1288163.

199. Marco Tosatti, "Ecco come andò davvero il Conclave del 2005," Vatican Insider, *La Stampa*, February 28, 2013, https://web.archive.org/web/20130304003525/http://vaticaninsider.lastampa.it/vaticano/dettaglio-articolo/articolo/conclave-22761/.

200. Alessandro Speciale, "Vatican Defends Pope Francis' Actions during Argentina's 'Dirty War,'" *Washington Post*, March 15, 2013, https://www.washingtonpost.com/national/on-faith/vatican-defends-pope-francis-actions-during-argentinasdirty-war/2013/03/15/070f5324-8db5-11e2-adca-74ab31da3399_story.html.

200. Vatican Insider, "Why Bergoglio Travels So Little," Vatican Insider, *La Stampa*, March 29, 2014, http://www.lastampa.it/2014/03/29/esteri/vatican-insider/en/why-bergoglio-travels-so-little-NbBzQ8c3DvALud1JCTH5HP/pagina.html.

200. "Bergoglio presenta la renuncia," *El Tribuno*, December 15, 2011, http://www.eltribuno.info/jujuy/nota/2011-12-15-21-47-0-bergoglio-presenta-la-renuncia.

203. Quoted in Philip Pullella, "Pope Attacks Mega-Salaries and Wealth Gap in Peace Message," Reuters, December 12, 2013, http://www.reuters.com/article/us-pope-economy-idUSBRE9BB0EH20131212.

204. Thomas Reese, "The Francis Effect," National Catholic Reporter, March 6, 2014, https://www.ncronline.org/blogs/faith-and-justice/francis-effect.

205. Ibid.

206. Ibid.

207. Tom Kington, "Conservative Opposition to Pope Francis Spurs Talk of a Schism in the Catholic Church," Los Angeles Times, April 17, 2017, http://www.latimes.com/world/europe/la-fg-pope-conservatives-2017-story.html.

208. Quoted in ibid.

208. Jeet Heer, "Do Conservative Catholics Want a Divorce?" New Republic, September 28, 2015, https://newrepublic.com/article/122945/why-are-some-conservative-catholics-talking-schism.

209. Quoted in ibid.

210. Ibid.

211. Quoted in ibid.

214. Peter Beaumont, "Pope Francis Offers Prayers at Israeli Separation Wall in Bethlehem," Guardian, May 25, 2014, https://www.theguardian.com/world/2014/may/25/pope-francis-israeli-separation-wall-bethlehem.

215. Ibid.

216. Barack Obama, "Statement by the President on Cuba Policy Changes," White House Office of the Press Secretary, December 17, 2014, https://obamawhitehouse.archives.gov/the-press-office/2014/12/17/statement-president-cuba-policy-changes.

218. Agence France-Presse, "Pope Francis: married men could be ordained to ease priest shortages," Guardian, March 10, 2017, https://www.theguardian.com/world/2017/mar/10/pope-francis-married-men-could-be-ordained-to-ease-priest-shortages.

218. Stephanie Kirchgaessner and Harriet Sherwood, "Pope Francis to consider ordaining women as deacons," Guardian, May 12, 2016, https://www.theguardian.com/world/2016/may/12/pope-francis-consider-ordaining-women-female-deacons-catholic-church-commission.

219. Christopher Lamb, "Change Catholic Teaching to Make Death Penalty 'Inadmissible', Says Pope," Tablet, October 12, 2017, http://www.thetablet.co.uk/news/7899/0/change-catholic-teaching-to-make-death-penalty-inadmissible-says-pope.

220. Neal Baker, "Weapons of Holy Mass Destruction: Pope Francis Wades into North Korea Crisis and Vows to Save the World from Nuclear Disaster," *Sun*, November 9, 2017, https://www.thesun.co.uk/news/4876328/pope-francis-north-korea-nuclear-latest-kim-jong-un/.

220. Associated Press, "Pope Francis to Address Nuclear Crisis at Vatican Conference," *USA Today*, November 10, 2017, https://www.usatoday.com/story/news/world/2017/11/10/pope-francis-nuclear-weapons-vatican-conference/851379001/.

221. Jason Horowitz, "Pope Francis Ousts Powerful Conservative Cardinal," *New York Times*, July 1, 2017, https://www.nytimes.com/2017/07/01/world/europe/vatican-pope-doctrine-mueller.html.

222. Sébastien Maillard, "How Long Francis Will Remain Pope—and What's Keeping Him in the Vatican," *Huffington Post*, accessed November 13, 2017, https://www.huffingtonpost.com/sebastien-maillard/pope-francis-remain-pope_b_9439638.html.

223. Maillard, "How Long Francis Will Remain Pope."

224. Michael J. O'Loughlin, "Pope Francis Says Give to the Homeless, Don't Worry About How They Spend It, as Lent Begins," *America*, February 28, 2017, https://www.americamagazine.org/politics-society/2017/02/28/pope-francis-says-give-homeless-dont-worry-about-how-they-spend-it-lent.

225. Ishaan Tharoor, "Trump Meets Pope Francis, His Antithesis," *Washington Post*, May 24, 2017, https://www.washingtonpost.com/news/worldviews/wp/2017/05/24/trump-meets-pope-francis-his-antithesis/.

226. Quoted in Katie Forster, "Pope Francis: There is 'No Point' Going to Church If You Don't Really Believe in It," *Independent*, January 16, 2017, http://www.independent.co.uk/news/world/europe/pope-francis-catholic-church-no-point-if-you-dont-believe-in-it-help-the-poor-christian-parrots-a7529631.html.

227. Quoted in Guillermoprieto, "Francis's Holy War."

228. Quoted in ibid.

ALSO BY TED RALL

"A dramatic, evocative, thoughtful and very accessible account of one of the most important stories of the century—and one of the most ominous, unless citizens are roused to action to rein in abusive state power."
—Noam Chomsky

$16.95 • ISBN: 978-1-60980-635-4

"More than a campaign biography, this graphic narrative traces the decline and possible resurgence of liberalism within the Democratic Party ... An effective primer on a strong voice from the left to counter the Democrats' rightward shift." —*Kirkus Reviews*

$16.95 • ISBN: 978-1-60980-698-9

Donald Trump, who never held political office, pulled off his ultimate acquisition: the hostile takeover of the Republican Party. Everyone was shocked—except those who knew him.

$16.95 • ISBN: 978-1-60980-758-0